PRAISE FOR

"Decision points on choosing, getting into and succeeding at college are skillfully arranged in this easy-to-use guidebook by a longtime teacher and administrator who also builds on the experience of guiding her own four children through the process.

As a former college administrator, Greta Oliver knows this subject from the inside and the outside (as the parent of four grown children). As the undergraduate dean in the Scripps College of Communication at Ohio University, I worked closely with Greta for years as we guided thousands of students through recruiting, deciding, securing financial aid, choosing courses and succeeding in them. Her expert guide is thorough, clearly written and a graphic marvel.

Greta Oliver's roadmap to the many steps of college success should be required reading for anyone planning to attend and to succeed in college. Think of it as a portable mini-encyclopedia of facts and advice at each step of the way in navigating a complex journey--all from an expert in both the academic and administrative crossroads in higher education. We worked together for years and spent hours untangling knots in the process for students and their families. I see those years culminating in this expert guidebook that I highly recommend."

-Dr. Florence Clark Riffe
Retired Assistant Dean for Undergraduate Programs and Services
Scripps College of Communication
Ohio University

"I, as a first-generation college attendee, would have benefited greatly from this valuable resource. It will be extremely helpful for students and families navigating the college application, admission process. I wish that I had access to such a resource when I was beginning my journey."

-Dr. Carolyn Jefferson-Jenkins
Adjunct Assistant Professor, School of Education
University of North Carolina at Chapel Hill

"I don't think I exaggerate when I say reading this book is like hitting the mother lode. Dr. Oliver pulls back that institutionalized curtain that overshadows the many pathways to a successful higher education journey. It's not a one-time read. Keep it on your shelf and refer to it throughout your college experience.

Yes, this book is for parents and their students considering college. It's also an essential read for those in the academy who interact and work with these parents and students. Dr. Oliver has been in all these roles, so she knows better than most what's involved and what's needed to succeed. In fact, she shares her personal experiences – warts and all. You will learn from the mistakes she, her husband and their children made. And, it's a comfortable read... like you are having a conversation with Dr. Oliver."

-Dr. Lois Boynton
Associate Professor, UNC Hussman School of Journalism and Media
University of North Carolina at Chapel Hill

"Dr. Oliver's book provides thoughtful and practical insights to guide both students and parents through the college matriculation process; from application to graduation. Students will find her tips to be helpful and easily applicable, regardless of the institution they choose to attend; and parents will find her advice helpful to invoke confidence and reassurance. This is an incredibly valuable resource!"

-Dr. Erin Almond
Senior Manager, KIPP Through College Program

"This brief book is loaded with wisdom and important reflections about navigating the process of college admissions. The guidance offered is worthwhile for future college students and their parents. These tips are practical, thoughtful and contain information that I wish I had when my daughters applied to college. Reading this book might help families avoid making errors in applying to and selecting a college. This book helps parents envision how to really be helpful to their children in making an important life decision about where and how to go to college."

-Dr. Ron Strauss
Executive Vice Chancellor and Provost
University of North Carolina at Chapel Hill

"Reflecting on my own college search process that began over 20 years ago, I now realize that my successful matriculation into higher education occurred despite, and not because of, the knowledge I brought to this process. I had a healthy support system; however, as a first-generation college student, I was totally ignorant to the college selection process and like the saying goes, I was unaware that I did not know. I had a gap in my college knowledge that could have jeopardized my ability to get into and be successful in college. Fortunately, I went to an exceptional public high school that had the resources to provide students with college and career counselors who were responsible for helping graduating seniors with their post-secondary planning.

What happens to individuals who lack the knowledge of the college search and are unaware of how to decipher if they can thrive at a particular university?

For families who lack an understanding of how to navigate the college search and subsequent choice process, *College Roadmap* fills this important lack of knowledge base. Providing excellent insight presented in the form of personal stories, "to do" lists, and countless examples, this book is an excellent resource for any family who has students who aspire to higher education. In providing a good blueprint for the selection process *College Roadmap* can take a complex and sometimes insurmountable process, and present a "how to" in a way that anyone can understand and follow. Perhaps the most unique component of this book is the intentional messaging provided by Dr. Oliver to all the different stakeholders involved in a potential student's sphere of influence during the search process. Dr. Oliver's ability to carve out unique roles and responsibilities for families, students, mentors, and other individuals ultimately confirms the belief held by many that "it takes a village" to assure the success of a college student. Perhaps the most useful resource to readers is the glossary of terms which provides the opportunity for anyone to become a cultural navigator in helping their students to be successful in college. This is an early must-read for anyone undergoing the college search process."

> *-Dr. Brandon H. Common*
> *Associate Vice President & Dean of Students*
> *Louisiana State University*

"This book is a gold mine, especially for first-generation college students and their families!"

> *-Kelly Davidson, M.Ed.*
> *Academic Advisor, Intervention Specialist Education Liaison*
> *Patton College of Education, Ohio University*

COLLEGE ROADMAP

ESSENTIAL TIPS FOR FIRST-TIME COLLEGE STUDENTS AND THEIR FAMILIES

DR. GRETA OLIVER

ISBN 978-1-7375089-0-8 (paperback[b])
ISBN 978-1-7375089-1-5 (Ebook)

Library of Congress Control Number: 2021913158

Printed in Chapel Hill, North Carolina, USA by Greta Thomas Oliver

This book is not intended for use as a source of legal, medical, accounting, or financial advice. All readers are advised to seek the services of competent professionals in the legal, medical, accounting, and financial fields.

The advice and strategies found within may not be suitable for every situation. This work is sold with the understanding that neither the author nor the publisher is held responsible for the results accrued from the advice in this book. Use of this book does not establish any type of advisory, coaching, counseling, or professional relationship with the author or publisher.

For bulk book orders, email Gretathomasoliver@gmail.com.

Photo Credits - Envato, Book design, cover designer, graphic illustration, Brittany Annis

For more information, visit www.GretaOliverConsulting.com.

Dedicated with love and sincere gratitude to the memory of my first cheerleader, my advocate and the greatest woman I have ever known, my mother, Denola Thomas.

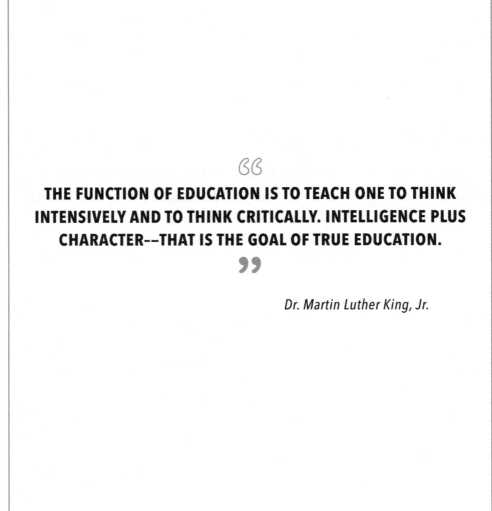

THE FUNCTION OF EDUCATION IS TO TEACH ONE TO THINK INTENSIVELY AND TO THINK CRITICALLY. INTELLIGENCE PLUS CHARACTER--THAT IS THE GOAL OF TRUE EDUCATION.

Dr. Martin Luther King, Jr.

ACKNOWLEDGMENTS

Many individuals helped with the development of laying out a plan to guide the college search for parents and their first-time students. I know the book is important because many of my friends and acquaintances are in the process of navigating this daunting task. After taking many late-night, last-minute calls from parents regarding this subject, I decided to write this book to allow others to get in front of this important endeavor. Individuals who contributed:

Dr. Erin Almond
Senior Manager, KIPP Through College Program

Brittany Annis
Designer and Illustrator

Dr. Lois Boynton
Associate Professor, UNC Hussman School of Journalism and Media
University of North Carolina at Chapel Hill

Kelly Davidson, M.Ed.
Academic Advisor, Intervention Specialist Education Liaison
Patton College of Education, Ohio University

Stephen Farmer
Vice Provost for Enrollment, University of Virginia

Darrel G. Greene
Website Developer

Dr. Carolyn Jefferson-Jenkins
Adjunct Assistant Professor, School of Education
University of North Carolina at Chapel Hill

Sandi Krivesti
Senior Assistant Director of Scholarships
Office of Student Financial Aid and Scholarships, Ohio University

Charlie Lehmann
SCORE Mentor

Dr. Trevy McDonald
Associate Professor, UNC Hussman School of Journalism and Media
University of North Carolina at Chapel Hill

Terence Oliver
Professor, UNC Hussman School of Journalism and Media
University of North Carolina at Chapel Hill
Simply Told Design

Kweneshia Price
Director of Aspiring Eagles Academy, Lead Academic Coach,
North Carolina Central University

Dr. Florence Riffe
Retired Assistant Dean for Undergraduate Programs and Services
Scripps College of Communication, Ohio University

Chris Roush
Dean, School of Communications, Quinnipiac University

Stuart Warner
Retired Editor of Phoenix New Times

Thank you also to many colleagues from the UNC Hussman School of Journalism and Media who offered ideas and support during the writing of this book including: Livis Freeman, Angelena King and Michael Gawlik; and the individuals to whom they connected me, Mary Towe and Jennifer Kohn. To the over 1,000 students I have had the pleasure of serving at two major universities, one college, and three high schools as a teacher, instructor, adjunct professor, mentor, advisor, assistant director, program coordinator, program co-director, program director, college representative, mentor and friend. It is for all of you that I write this book, as well as for all of the students to come.

SPECIAL ACKNOWLEDGEMENT

A special thank you to Dr. Donovan Livingston, who was so gracious to write the foreword for this book. Livingston is an award-winning educator, spoken word poet and public speaker who has been featured worldwide. He is a consummate student, educator and believer in the enormous opportunities provided by higher education, and he is more than qualified to write the foreword and to invite students and their parents to experience higher education opportunities for themselves. Drawing on his personal experiences, Livingston inspires students, educators, and communities with his conviction that all children have the potential and right to "lift off" and fly in pursuit of their dreams. Dr. Livingston has earned master's degrees from Columbia University and Harvard University, and received his doctorate degree from UNC Greensboro.

MY REASON WHY

I was not ready for college!

It was September 6, 1975. With my overstuffed bags and boxes stacked in my room and the glare of the sun forcing itself through the window, I watched my parents slowly exit the parking lot of Kreischer-Compton Quadrangle on the campus of Bowling Green State University. I felt like I was in the middle of nowhere.

A deep sense of abandonment overshadowed my soul. I was alone, woefully ill-prepared for college life, and afraid of what the future would hold for me. My thoughts shifted to my parents. I was sure they also felt uncertainty and perhaps even fear about how this would all unfold.

I was an African-American, first-generation college student (FGCS) at a predominantly white institution (PWI). My parents were not college graduates, in fact, no one in my entire family was. My family had sacrificed for me to be here. My mother was working overtime to help pay for my education. Since they'd never had this experience, they were as in the dark about the college process and what to expect as I was.

As the first person in my family to go away to college, many eyes and hopes were on me. Would I make the transition successfully or would I disappoint them and be sent home in disgrace? I could not erase from my mind the hope for my future in my parents' eyes as they pushed me toward the goal of higher education.

Back then, there was no guidebook explaining the college process to parents or new students. There was no internet, limited resources, and very few, if any, role models or mentors around to help students and parents navigate this journey from start to finish. We were left to figure it out on our own, the hard way.

College Roadmap: Essential Tips for First-Time College Students and Their Families is the roadmap that will help students and their families navigate the path from prospective college student to college graduate with less stress, more ease, and without experiencing the many pitfalls along the road.

I've come a long way since those days at Bowling Green State University. As I look back, I realize that some of my most fulfilling experiences have been helping students reach their goals of higher education. My hope is that I can provide a helping hand on their journey, that I make an impact and a difference for both them and their parents.

Years later, as a college administrator, I worked closely with hundreds of students in varying roles such as program director, coordinator, adjunct instructor, scholarship advisor, and scholarship director, among other things. I definitely wanted the students with whom I worked to know that I was there should they need assistance. It is my hope that my experience and tips shared here in *College Roadmap* can make the preparation to college more smooth and less stressful.

As a college administrator I exhibited "tough love," advising and supporting my students and I was constantly reaching out to them. My office door was always open and I became the advocate that I wished I'd had during my undergrad experience. Over the years I have mentored many students, provided many letters of recommendation, and worked closely with graduate students and work-study students, providing support whenever and wherever I could. It is my joy to maintain relationships with many of these students and witness their successes since graduation.

I believe in education being a game-changer for individuals and families. Education changed my life and it offered me a different vantage point from which to help first-year students. In my experience, I have found that many students coming to college are ill-prepared to meet the challenge of higher education. Preparation is key for success in this journey and starts before any student steps foot on campus. It is my hope that you can use and appreciate all that is presented here to help you begin preparing for your journey to college, and that you will persist and reach your goal of graduation. I want to help students reach their goal of higher education. This is my reason why.

SPECIAL GIFT FROM DR. OLIVER

Choosing a college and going away to school can be confusing and stressful for both parents and the student.

When you finish this book, you'll be armed with what you need to know about finding a college that fits, what to do as you are waiting for admission decisions, how to set yourself up for success, where to ask for help on campus, and how to navigate the journey from prospective college student to college graduate. The tips provided in this book are for both prospective students and their families and will enable each of you to understand the process and stay organized throughout the journey.

You'll also receive the special bonus I created to add to your toolkit, the Roadmap Essentials, which are 5 downloadable forms that will prove invaluable during college visits, as you work to secure financial aid, and as you compare one institution with another.

While these working papers are offered for sale, as a special bonus you can claim it for free at https://www.gretaoliverconsulting.com/gift.

The sooner you apply the essential tips inside this book, the better your chances for successfully creating and following your personal roadmap to higher education success.

I'm in your corner. Let me know if I can help further.

Here's to finding your way through this key process with more ease and less stress.

Best,

CONTENTS

TO THE PARENTS - BEFORE THE SEARCH

One of the most daunting tasks for a parent is undertaking the process of finding a college for your child. Once you are over the shock that your child is no longer a baby, you find that you are thrust into the world of exploring colleges with your teen. This is no easy process, but with organization and a guide, it can be done with minimal stress. The task of finding a college can be especially overwhelming if your child is a first-generation college student, or if you attended college but have been away from college for some time. This book is designed to help you navigate the waters and to help you become organized in your search for a college that fits, where your student can be comfortable and thrive. I know from experience what you are going through as a parent and have walked in your shoes. As a mother of four adults who all attended college, with three of the four graduating from college, and as a former student development professional and adjunct professor who worked as an administrator and educator at two large universities as well as a community college, I have had the opportunity to work with students from the freshman to graduate student level including those of traditional and non-traditional ages. This book outlines what it takes from my experience to make the college search process and the transition to college easier. Additionally, my work alongside students as a professional has provided me with tips and strategies to help students persist in higher education. Also included are comments from higher education professionals whose expertise helped shape this book. I hope you will take this information to heart and that you will find it useful as a parent of a student entering the world of higher education.

TO THE STUDENT - BEFORE THE SEARCH

If you have plans to go to college, hopefully you have already started preparations toward doing so. It's important that you find a college where you can feel comfortable. Additionally, it is important that you explore all your options before you get to college in order to make the transition from high school to college as painless as possible.

You will find that the environment at college will be different from anything you've experienced before. Most of you will find yourselves away from home for the first time. You'll be expected to be independent, to make your own decisions and to be responsible. This book is an effort to help you as you enter into the world of higher education. Remember that even as a college student away from home, you have advocates. Find your advocates and allow others to help you. Do not be afraid to ask for help. You can persist. You can obtain a higher education. Best wishes to you as you embark on this new, exciting adventure.

FOREWORD
Dr. Donovan A. Livingston

In an increasingly interconnected, rapidly evolving world, information is currency. And those who have capital also hold power. It is a power that is safeguarded by privilege, wealth and the long, ceaseless story of systemic oppression in these United States. On the surface, access to information seems circumstantial, even apolitical. In a culture that demands one lift themselves by their bootstraps, we deride the uninformed, seemingly blaming them for their own oppression, justifying their inability to escape intergenerational cycles of poverty. However, upon peeling back the layers of American history, we are compelled to ask ourselves, as conscientious participants in a democratic society, why so many among us lack the information necessary to navigate those systems that dictate American life. To that end, the pursuit of the American Dream – insofar as we believe in such a thing – historically, has been linked to educational opportunity. It is no coincidence that as America became more meritocratic, economic mobility, too, became a natural byproduct of college degree attainment. Simply put, as one acquires academic credentials, so, too, do they establish a semblance of financial stability. Thus, as a recent college graduate – wide-eyed and idealistic – I entered two urban Title I high schools as a college advisor, with the promise of educational opportunity on my breath. What I lacked in experience, I made up for in accessibility. I worked closely with students and families to ensure they understood the nuances of the college application process and the utility of postsecondary schooling. From leading campus tours and FAFSA® workshops to incorporating intrusive advising practices, I was deeply invested in the process of seeing my students – most of whom were from historically underrepresented populations in higher education – and their families through the uncertainty and excitement of applying to college.

For all the investments I made however, my earliest missteps as an educator involved my approach to advising, parroting talking points like, "college graduates earn about one million more dollars in their lifetime than high school graduates." Although such refrains were empirically accurate, it was as if my college-access pedagogy was grounded in capitalism, rather than a commitment to lifelong learning. Thus, reading Dr. Oliver's *College Roadmap: Essential Tips for First Time College Students and Their Families* was, for me, a return to those long but fulfilling days of fee waivers, field trips, essays and SAT registrations. It was a reminder that there was more to enrolling and completing college than finding a job and securing a living wage. While we agree that attending college might not necessarily be appropriate for everyone, Dr. Oliver equips her audience with the information necessary to successfully navigate the application process, should one choose to do so.

On the surface, it may seem as if college acceptance is the sole purpose of this project. While that sentiment is correct, it is true, only in part. A deeper look into the text reveals something more endearing, almost everlasting about what a college experience has to offer, for both students and their families. Dr. Oliver insists that one's admittance to an institution of higher education is but a small step in the journey to self. She implores students to think critically about what they hope to accomplish within and beyond the classroom, and how to care for themselves - socially, emotionally, and financially - upon arriving at the college of their choosing. Her message is as convenient as it is accessible, which is a true testament to her gift as an educator. After all, the language of college enrollment is technical and, at times, just confusing enough to misinform, discourage, and deter historically underrepresented students in higher education from engaging with the application process. While Dr. Oliver's expertise is on full display, she offers cautionary tales of her own children, and their (mis)management of the transition from high school to college. Such insight into her own experiences as a student and parent are both humanizing and disarming, reminding us to embrace vulnerability as an essential component of what it truly means to be college ready. If information is currency, then this text is itself a form of legal tender: an investment in the lives of students and families who historically have been marginalized within the American education machine. Although the hope of educational equity requires collective work, *College Roadmap: Essential Tips for First Time College Students and Their Families*, lights the way for individual students and families to dismantle the ivory tower, brick by brick.

INTRODUCTION

So Your Kid is Ready for College, Now What?

BEFORE THE SEARCH

It seems like only yesterday that you were putting your kid on the school bus for the first day of kindergarten. You are wondering where the time went. How is it time to go to college? Believe it or not, the time has come, and you probably have not started the college search process. What do you do now?

Looking for and finding a college for your student takes a great deal of work. It can seem like there are simply too many choices. This book will help you narrow the search, make the process of finding a school easier and more efficient and provide useful information that your student can use once they arrive on campus.

But first, talk to your student and find out their reasons why they want to pursue a higher education. If you find that a higher education is not in your student's future, you may want to pick up another book that will outline how to explore the job market after graduation.

> **ONCE THE 'WHY' OF ATTENDING COLLEGE IS DETERMINED, YOU CAN PREPARE TO BEGIN THE SEARCH**

Once the "why" of attending college is determined, you can prepare to begin the search. The earlier you start the better. Keep in mind that even if your student does find various possible college options, he or she has to gain admittance to the college--they must be accepted. You really don't want to wait until the last minute.

Colleges base their admission on various criteria. Each college is different. In general, community colleges, which are two-year institutions that typically award program completion certificates and associate degrees (two-year degrees), are easier to get into. The mission of community colleges includes access. They were established so that students would be able to attend them readily, and usually there are many to choose from that are close to home.

Additionally, if applicants apply to a four-year institution but fail to get accepted, they can usually attend an accredited two-year college and transfer into the four-year institution later. Of course, applicants would be wise to discuss if credits for courses that they take at the two-year institution are transferable to the four-year institution. Attaining a two-year college degree (associate's) and then transferring to a four-year institution is a good choice for those who were initially denied admission to a four-year institution, or for those who want to save money.

Talking with your student and determining what type of institution they are interested in attending will help you save both time and energy.

What are the attributes of a great college? Stay tuned for some helpful hints to find a place that fits!

PART 1
BEFORE THE SEARCH

FINDING A COLLEGE THAT "FITS"

Have you ever been in a place where you just feel great? The atmosphere is nice, the social climate is pleasant and the people seem like they enjoy where they are and what they're doing? College "fit" is something like that. Fit basically is how you feel in a particular place. Is the place welcoming? Do you feel safe and secure in the surroundings? Fit can also be attributed to the accessibility of a place. Are you able to navigate from place to place without feeling overwhelmed?

One of the most important things that you'll need not only to survive but thrive at your college is a good sense of fit. This is one of the reasons why college visits are so important. It is much easier to gauge fit if you are physically in a place and are able to move about in the space. When you are on campus, pay attention to the climate of the place. How it makes you feel personally is vitally important. Does the environment feel welcoming or hostile? Are the people friendly? Do the students seem happy and fulfilled? Do employees seem open and inviting? How are the buildings maintained? Can you easily navigate the campus? Are directional signs clear or confusing? A bad fit is often a major reason why students don't finish. If you find that you don't have a good fit with your university, you are likely to feel isolated and depressed. You need to have a sense of community in your new environment. You will be spending the majority of your time at the university that you choose for several years. You need to feel comfortable.

Ultimately during your college visits, you will want to determine if the environment is nurturing and if you can envision spending years in the setting. Can you picture yourself living in the residence halls, walking across campus to class, eating in the dining halls, walking across the stage to receive your degree? Will you thrive or barely survive?

WILL YOU THRIVE OR BARELY SURIVE?

"

Disclaimer: Sometimes students are not able to search for fit on the campus they ultimately attend. In the case of student athletes or other students who are recruited to a campus for specific scholarships or special programs such as high school to college pipeline programs, they are being offered an opportunity to attend in the form of an athletic or academic scholarship. If your student falls into this category, it is my hope that they at least feel good about the decision that they have made and can find their way in the setting they have chosen.

Fit, or a feeling of belongingness, can also be tied to a particular type of college or university. When thinking in general terms about where you might be most comfortable, as a member of the majority, a student might feel more comfortable at a predominantly white institution, whereas a student of color might want to consider a historically black college or university. Additionally, the size of the institution and the faculty-to-student ratio is also very important. The applicant will need to closely evaluate which type and size university best suits them, where they feel most comfortable and where they feel the atmosphere is most conducive to learning.

For some students, other types of institutions or scenarios may work better. There are many different options for consideration such as trade (specialized) schools, training centers, working for a business and so on.

If you are still reading this book, it is safe to assume that your student is interested in attending college. This is a very important decision and must be made for the right reasons. Your student should desire to attend college for themselves and not for anyone else. Too often students are thrust into the college setting to satisfy or fulfill the dreams and desires of others, such as their parents, rather than themselves. A student who is entering the world of higher education has a great deal of work ahead of them and it starts with a proper mindset! If your student is not interested in college or does not have the proper attitude about college attendance, their road will be especially hard. Before starting down the path of higher education, make sure that your student is on the path for themselves. It is vitally important to the student that they want to be there. If so, then let's go!

TIP 1 - BE AN EARLY BIRD
Start the Search Early

There is an old proverb that says, "the early bird catches the worm." In the case of starting the search for college, it is never too early. The sooner, the better! Below are some ideas you can incorporate to get the college search underway.

1. You can start the process by encouraging your student to attend college fairs to pick up brochures/pamphlets about specific colleges. Visit nacacnet.org to find listings of college fairs.

2. Use Google to look up colleges both near and far (remember: out-of-state rates are higher than in-state and private colleges are more expensive than public colleges).

3. Visit your local library to search for books about colleges your student is interested in.

4. Go to the webpage of the college your student is interested in and download and view their college catalog. Take note of the types of classes your student will be required to take for their desired major. Encourage your student to check out a course description book and to be sure to make note of prerequisites and other requirements that may be listed for specific classes of interest. Create a tentative schedule starting with the minimum credit-hour load that can be taken to begin. It is best to start with fewer courses than to become overwhelmed with too many credit hours and classes before finding out how rigorous college courses can be.

5. If your student is undecided and has not yet determined a major, review the general education requirements (the courses that all students have to complete regardless of major). Take note of substitutions that can be made for particular courses, if applicable.

6. Encourage your student to speak to their high school counselor about

the college search process as early as possible. Disclaimer: In many school districts, the student-to-counselor ratio is extremely high, meaning that students are not able to readily meet with their assigned counselor or receive helpful services in a timely manner, if at all. Please note that when I advise students to utilize school counselors as a resource, this may not be a viable option in some cases. In such instances, parents and students will be better served researching solutions on their own. Because of this reality in many of the nation's high schools, I spoke with several counselors in the writing of this book. I found the counselors very busy but more than willing to help all students assigned to them as best as they possibly can.

7. Become aware of early admission deadlines at various universities. Since your student may be interested in several colleges, be sure to take organized notes regarding deadlines for each.

ECONOMICAL TIP

Applying to college is expensive. Applicants are expected to pay an application fee when applying to most universities, and the money is not refundable if your student is not admitted or chooses to go elsewhere. Colleges in some states have special time periods reserved when they do not require an application fee. Find out from the admissions department of the college you are researching about their specific guidelines. ASK if a fee waiver is available. This will allow your student to apply to a specific institution without paying the application fee. Note: There is a big difference between in-state and out-of-state tuition rates. Students attending a university that is located in a state other than the state in which they are living can expect to pay dearly for it. College Board reports that the average cost for a year of out-of-state tuition and fees is $23,890 annually, while the average cost of in-state tuition is $9,410. Check out the costs of each university you wish to attend to make sure you are aware of all of the costs before investing your time into the search (collegeboard.org).

TIP 2 - PREPARE FOR ADMISSIONS TESTS
Find Resources and Get Started as Early as Possible

Find out which admission tests are required at the universities your student is applying to. Note: some institutions do not require admissions tests, but most do. Sign your student up for SAT and ACT prep sessions or classes. Research both tests because they test the same things in different ways. Check out the SAT at collegeboard.com and the ACT at actstudent.org. Typically students will do better on one test than the other. Have your student visit the local library for SAT/ACT study materials or pick up a study book from the local bookstore. Have your student

TESTING

visit their high school counselor to see if they have study books for the tests that can be borrowed. Prepare your student that they may have to take each test multiple times for the best possible score. Encourage your student to study and prepare for admissions tests constantly. There are many different study aids that your student can take advantage of to increase their chances of getting a better score. Check at your student's high school to see if they have any after school test prep sessions available for students who are scheduled to take the test. If your student needs tutoring for the tests, secure a tutor or test prep coach as early as you can.

ECONOMICAL TIP

Research SAT and ACT test fee waivers. Sometimes if your student is a member of a certain student program, like Upward Bound or AVID, they can take one or more of the tests without paying a fee. Look into college readiness programs at your student's high school at the beginning of their high school career (ninth grade).

The PSAT (Preliminary SAT) is a great practice test that can be taken by students in the 10th and 11th grade. The test measures readiness for college, provides for scholarship access and is great practice for the SAT. Students can take the test once a year in both the 10th and 11th grade. Initial scores received on the PSAT can provide a good indication of where a student stands in the subject areas tested and provide a basis for further strategic study for the upcoming SAT. If your student meets income eligibility requirements, have them speak to their high school counselor or a representative of a community-based organization to obtain a fee waiver in advance of taking the test.

For SAT/ACT testing, students can receive access to free prep online. Collegeboard works with Khan Academy, and after students take the PSAT, they can receive SAT prep based on their PSAT scores. The best thing about this test preparation is that the help provided is based on the participants' individual scores and weaknesses. Additionally, when students register for the ACT, they gain access to ACT Academy, which is the ACT online prep mechanism. Both of these opportunities are free! The Khan Academy is a non-profit educational organization that provides free video tutorials and interactive exercises. The Academy's declared mission is "changing education for the better by providing a free world-class education to anyone anywhere." Check out The Khan Academy by going to their website at KhanAcademy.org.

TIP 3 - WRITE YOUR APPLICATION ESSAY

An admission essay is so important in today's climate as you prepare your application materials. As a result of the COVID-19 global pandemic, some universities have chosen to forego standardized test scores and student organization membership as criteria on the part of prospective students because neither option had been available for over a year as many students completed their studies at home. In lieu of standardized test scores and other admissions criteria, a well-written admission essay can be the very thing that differentiates you from other prospective students.

Fact: Scores on standardized tests are being used less and less for admission decisions at universities, either by weighting them less in algorithms or not requiring the scores at all. The essay you write therefore may have more impact than ever before in whether you pass muster.

Below are some things that you should keep in mind as you are formulating your application essay.

■ **DON'T DO THIS**

> Don't list accomplishments found elsewhere on your application or resume. (You'll insult the readers of your packet who have already read your accomplishments, which–by the way–are very similar to all the other applicants).

> Don't say why you have your heart set on that particular college or university. (You will not sound genuine, especially if you can replace the name of the institution and substitute another and be just as convincing).

Don't predict the great things you will accomplish in the future, or even hope to accomplish. (Leave your crystal ball out of a rational discussion.)

Don't ask anyone for help. (The admission office will never know you did, but it's cheating just as much as copying someone else's essay would be. If you can't choose and write about a topic that fits you, you may not be ready for college).

■ DO THIS

Write about an event that happened to you that changed you in some way–morally, educationally, socially–and explain how it contributed to your maturity.

Teach the reader something new you've learned recently through combining reading and research with observation that led you to change your mind on a topic.

Write both pro and con arguments on a topic that has always troubled you.

Write and rewrite your essay a dozen times. Polish it some more. When you think it is finished and only then, show it to someone who has known you all your life and ask: "Does this essay describe me accurately?"

TIP 4 - GATHER INFORMATION
Research Any University Your Student Is Interested in Attending

THE SEARCH

Along with your student, check the fact book of any institution your student is interested in visiting. To do so, go to the webpage of the institution. In the search box type "fact book," and view the contents of the fact book to find out useful information about the university before your visit to campus. The fact book will contain information including the profile of the current freshman class, their average GPA, test scores and demographics. This information will give you an idea of how your student measures up to other students already admitted to the institution.

TIP 5 - DETERMINE INTERESTS

If your student already knows or has an idea of what their major course of study will be, great! If not, it's okay. However, you should encourage your student to familiarize themselves with the options available at institutions of interest. Be sure not to put any effort into institutions that do not offer majors that are of interest.

ECONOMICAL TIP

If your student is undecided, it might be a good idea for them to attend an accredited community college to complete their general education requirements and then transfer to a four-year institution (cheaper, too).

TIP 6 - TAKE COLLEGE TOURS
Investigate Schools that Offer Majors Your Student Is Interested in Pursuing

SCHEDULE COLLEGE VISITS

Check out the websites of the colleges you are interested in visiting. Look on the admissions page and take note of the dates of undergraduate admissions campus visit programs, as well as the time of campus tours and information about other recruitment activities. Check for opportunities for visits with
your student's school, church or other organizations. Get on campus. This is extremely important to the well-being of your student. While on campus, your student needs to look for fit. As mentioned earlier, fit is a feeling as much as anything else. Before the visit to campus, it might be a good idea for your student to check with their school counselor to see if there are any admitted high school alumni on campus at the university. If they have a connection there with someone they actually know, it will go a long way toward helping them feel more at home on campus and may result in a student-led campus tour. While you are on campus with your student, there are some specific things that should be done.

Walk the campus if possible. If your student is unable to connect with a friend from high school in advance for a personal tour, contact the admissions department for a tour. Most universities schedule several tours per day for prospective students and their families. While on the tour, take in the scenery. Pay attention to the signage as you go. Are there signs directing you to specific buildings or sections of college? How easy is the campus to navigate? Encourage your student to time themselves to see how long it takes to get from one side of the campus to another. While walking around visually check to see if the buildings and grounds are handicap accessible. While this might not be an issue for your student personally, it is definitely an indication of how committed the institution is to access and inclusion. If you are unable to tour the campus with a tour guide, pick up a map of the campus at the admissions office and go on a self-guided tour.

If the campus is not walkable, try out the bus system or whatever system is in place for students to get from place to place. Get off the bus and conduct your walking search as described above. Get into a classroom or two. If classes are in session, ask the professor for permission to quietly sit in the back and observe. Watch the interaction between the students and the professor. While this observation will not necessarily reflect what every class is like, it will give you an indication of the climate of the particular classroom you visit. Talk to students and professors. Are they welcoming and friendly? Check out the college bookstore. What is the ratio of college gear to actual books for sale? Explore the library. Is it open and inviting? Are there study rooms available? Is it brightly lit and is the temperature properly set? Are librarians visible? Is there an area with printers and copy machines for student use? Check out the extensive list of questions to ask and places to visit while on a college visit in the **WORKING PAPERS** section in the back of this book.

As the mother of four adult children, I've been on my share of college visits. I have even participated in preparing college visit programs for many prospective students on two college campuses over the years. Somehow, though, it was a bit different when I found myself on a college tour with one of my own. On one such visit, my husband, my oldest daughter and I went to visit an HBCU in Ohio. I did not attend an HBCU, so I was excited to get on campus to compare my past experiences with what I thought would be a totally different one. I had done a bit of research about the differences or perceived differences between the three PWIs that I attended while obtaining my degrees and the HBCU that I was visiting. I was honestly more interested in the college that we were visiting than my daughter was. My daughter was always very sensitive, and I had heard that the environment at most HBCUs was supposedly more nurturing than PWIs. After discussing this information with my husband, we were all set for the visit.

We began planning the visit. My daughter seemed somewhat afraid. She invited a high school friend to accompany us to the campus, which was about two hours away from our home. When we got on campus, we walked around and experienced the environment. The campus was alive with activity. When talking to the staff and professors on campus, they seemed inviting and said all the right things. When the band played it was just like watching the movie, *Drumline*. There was so much excitement going on. We went to the dining hall and the food was incredible. I wondered if the food would be as good every day if my daughter decided to attend. All in all, I deemed the visit a success. The environment seemed nurturing, the campus was easy to navigate, the staff seemed welcoming, the atmosphere was vibrant and exciting and the food was great. It seemed like a good place for my daughter.

> ## SHE WAS UNCOMFORTABLE AT A UNIVERSITY THAT I THOUGHT SHOULD HAVE FIT HER NEEDS

The problem was that my daughter hated it. She felt strange on the campus. She did not feel like there was a fit. She could not envision herself there. Bottom line, she was uncomfortable on a campus and at a university that I thought should have fit her needs. In the end, she said "no" to the university and we went on to visit others. Her friend said "yes" and went on to attend the university because it was a fit for her.

"
YOU NEED TO BE ABLE TO SEE YOURSELF THERE,
SEE YOURSELF NOT ONLY SURVIVING, BUT THRIVING
"

As a prospective student, it is important that regardless of what your parents feel, or what others feel, that the university you choose represents a "fit" for you. You need to be able to see yourself there, see yourself not only surviving, but thriving. Your being able to envision your new environment as your home for the next four or more years is key to your future success on campus.

My youngest daughter also took part in a few college visits of her own. My husband and I took her to my undergraduate alma mater for a visit. I was so excited to show her the campus where many years ago I received my undergraduate degree in Education. When we arrived, I scanned the small college town for differences that had occurred since my last visit over 30 years prior. Of course, many changes had occurred over the years. We pulled into the parking lot and started walking. She had an interview on campus for a scholarship and she also had been listed as a "prospective legacy admit" by the admissions office. As she interviewed, my husband and I walked the campus that we would later explore with her. It was especially cold. The wind blew between buildings as we sought shelter from the icy air. My mind went back to how brutal the winters had been in this small Ohio town and how students often cut through buildings when walking from place to place on campus for that very reason. One change that I noticed were bus stops on campus! What an improvement.

Once my daughter completed her on-campus interview, we toured more and she commented over and over about the cold weather. It was really cold, but somehow I wanted her to love the campus and feel comfortable in possibly attending. She did not. Even though she did receive a partial scholarship from the university and had been officially admitted, she ended up choosing another university that offered her a full-ride academic scholarship. She did not find "fit" on the campus I attended, but it was okay with me. She made her own decision based on her feelings of comfort and fit and not my desire to see her graduate from the college I attended, and she was right—it was cold.

ATTEND SUMMER PROGRAMS

Many campuses have summer programs for prospective students to get on campus before their senior year of high school. These programs usually have a specific focus or are tied to a particular college major. I personally had the pleasure of participating in a few of the many programs offered at Ohio University, including Future Communicators Day, Scripps College of Communications' Journalism Bootcamp and Ohio's named scholars campus visits, as well as the University of North Carolina's Chuck Stone Program, Upward Bound Summer Program and McNair Scholars Summer Program. In the case of both of these universities where I was employed, the goal was for prospective students to get on campus to see what campus life was about before hopefully becoming a student there. While the programs just mentioned were specific to those particular universities, there are many programs in place on campuses across the country which are designed to get students on campuses to see what it is really like to be up close and personal on a college campus. Seek out opportunities for your student to experience as many chances to get on the campuses that they are interested in before making a final college choice.

TIP 7 - UNDERSTAND FINANCIAL AID
Talk to Financial Aid Officers at Each Institution Your Student Is Considering

On your tour or at another designated time, be sure to stop into the financial aid office to speak with a professional about how financial aid awards are made at the institution of interest. One of the most important pieces of information that you will need to know is the specific cost of attendance for each  institution you are considering. In the meantime, do your part, which means filling out the Free Application for Federal Student Aid, commonly known as the FAFSA®, at the appropriate time, setting up a profile on FASTWEB (online resource in finding scholarships to help pay for school) and researching additional monies on your own. Once you determine the cost of attendance at the institution, you can plug in specific grants and scholarships that are being offered, plug in the amount your family can contribute and determine what to do about any gaps.

Specific questions you should ask while visiting the Financial Aid Office on your campus visit are:

1. What are my next steps after filling out the FAFSA®, registering on FASTWEB and researching scholarships with my family?

2. If I do receive assistance from this university, how will disbursement be made?

3. Are there any stipulations to receiving financial aid that I need to be aware of?

4. How can I be sure that I remain eligible for any financial aid I might receive?

5. If I do not meet the criteria at the end of the semester and lose my aid, what recourse, if any, do I have?

In addition to speaking directly with financial aid officers, check out the financial aid webpage of each university you are considering. There will be a great deal of information online regarding cost of attendance and priority deadline dates that you will need to take note of and adhere to.

Make sure that you understand the method(s) by which any scholarship monies will be applied. Since all institutions are different you can expect that the bills generated will vary. Understanding the terminology that is found on the invoices is vitally important. How monies, whether in the form of grants, scholarships, loans or other credits, are applied is important to know since whatever is not covered will become the responsibility of the family.

The following definitions should be fully understood by any financial aid recipient:

TUITION OR INSTRUCTIONAL FEES
These fees usually refer to the actual costs associated with providing instruction to the student. This amount will vary by the amount of courses (credit hours) taken per term.

GENERAL EXPENSES (FEES)
These fees usually cover additional costs that are not explained elsewhere on the bill.

TECHNOLOGY FEES
Fees associated with courses that are taken that require use of a computer lab.

ROOM AND BOARD OR HOUSING FEE
These fees are associated with a student being assigned to an on-campus residence hall and meal plan (in some instances, the room and board fees will be separated on the invoice).

Other fees you can expect to see are **health center fees, library fees, registrar fees, and activity fees**.

ADVICE FROM

CAROLINA COLLEGE ADVISING CORPS ADVISORS

Carolina College Advising Corps shared its advice for students and parents navigating the college search process for the first time.

ASK A LOT OF QUESTIONS
All of your questions are valid! Admissions counselors, college advisors, etc., are paid to help you, so please utilize them.

START CONNECTING EARLY
Connect with a college advisor or counselor before the senior year.

TOUR COLLEGES DURING THE SCHOOL YEAR
Talk with your counselor and see if your school offers a certain number of excused absences per year so that you can go tour colleges. Even if your school doesn't have field trips, you can still make time to visit schools, which is super helpful in the college exploration process!

SEEK ANSWERS TOGETHER
Don't expect your child to have all of the answers right away when it comes to looking/applying to colleges. Starting out, they are just as in the dark as you are. Seek out the answers together, so you're both on the same page.

UNDERSTAND INTERESTS
Use some sort of interest inventory to think about careers/majors and look for schools with similar programs.

USE THE COLLEGE BOARD'S BIG FUTURE WEBSITE
Visit www.bigfuture.org.

TOUR COLLEGES ON VACATION
Incorporate college tours into vacations (sounds lame, but even just driving through a campus on the way to the beach to give ninth or 10th graders an idea of what college even looks like can make a big difference).

CONSIDER ALL THE FACTORS
Always know that your child does not have to attend an Ivy League school in order to be an Ivy League student. The focus should be on what the school can provide the student and what is best for the student and/or family rather than what other students are doing/where they are committing. Some examples of consideration are: tuition, financial aid (loans, grants, scholarships), resources, environment and safety. Don't settle with just any school and know your worth. Stay out of debt! If that means going to school local/in-state or applying for scholarships every weekend, then do it. It's better to type a few short essays for a few weeks or months and receive free money than to spend 10+ years paying back loans.

DISCUSS FUTURE GOALS
Ask your student where they see themselves in their mid-20s to 30s. This way you can know if a four-year, two-year, or even a certificate is necessary.

STAY POSITIVE
Don't be discouraged. The process can be long and hard. Reach out to anyone credible (college advisors, counselors, admissions officers, etc.).

REACH OUT TO CURRENT/FORMER STUDENTS
Talk with current upperclassmen/recent graduates of colleges to get an idea of what the school is really like. They have clarity and honesty to their insight.

DON'T BE AFRAID OF ASKING QUESTIONS
Many parents/students have expressed a fear that asking questions of admissions counselors or calling the admissions office will make them seem "dumb." They are afraid that their application will somehow be penalized because they asked too many questions. This is not true! You deserve to have all the information when helping your student choose a college. Sending a quick email to the admissions office is a great way to get your questions answered, and it will not be held against parents/students.

SUPPORT AND NURTURE GOALS
When parents search for colleges with their student, they should first think of what their student wants to do. After that, they should look at schools that have majors and careers that align with those goals. If their student doesn't know what they want to do, they should look for colleges that have multiple majors/opportunities within a broad spectrum. They should also understand that even though they may have an idea of what their student wants to do, only their student will truly know. It's important to support their student's decisions and listen to their needs at the time. Have an opinion but know that ultimately the decision should be the student's.

ADHERE TO DEADLINES
Know your student's deadlines! Start very early and make a spreadsheet/calendar with every college, each scholarship application and the associated deadlines as soon as you find out about them.

EVALUATE DEBT AND MAKE WISE DECISIONS
Evaluate debt. A parent plus loan (a federal loan that parents of dependent undergraduate students can use to help pay for college or career school) is not required to receive a degree.

DON'T DISCOUNT COMMUNITY COLLEGES
Community colleges have a lot of merit, especially for students who have financial concerns. As mentioned earlier, they can also be useful if your student is undecided,

allowing them to take their general education requirements and transfer to another university at a later date if they so desire.

■ BE AWARE OF AVERAGE STUDENT STATISTICS
Look at prospective colleges' average GPA and ACT scores.

■ ADVOCATE FOR YOURSELF
Students: Advocating for yourself is one of the most helpful strategies. College and support staff (counselors, admissions reps, teachers, recommenders, etc.) want to hear from and help you, so use your voice!

■ KEEP AN OPEN MIND
Keep your mind open to new opportunities, fields of study, etc. You might find a great program that you would have never considered otherwise.

■ START THINKING EARLY
Think about your interests and skills before your senior year starts. There are so many schools to choose from and it can feel very overwhelming, but that list gets a lot smaller once you start to consider the location, size of the school, types of majors they have, etc.

■ IT'S OKAY TO BE UNSURE
Even though it seems like the world is forcing you to make your life decisions before you even graduate high school, it's okay to not know what you want to do or where you want to go. When you enter college, you will have so many different experiences and meet so many different people that doors will open that you may have never expected.

■ HAVE SEVERAL OPTIONS
Do everything you can to have as many options available as possible when it comes time to make a decision. Apply to as many things as you can! You never know where your head will be a couple of months down the road and you want to have as many doors open as possible.

■ IT'S OKAY TO CHANGE YOUR MIND
It's okay to change your mind, to not have all of the answers or to be confused. Just make sure that whatever you're doing, going forward, best aligns with who you are today and who you are working to become tomorrow.

■ FOLLOW YOUR PASSION
Love what you do! There are so many more important paths than just being a doctor, lawyer or engineer. There's so much pressure to fit into these categories, but it might not be the best fit for you! Think outside the box. Think about how you want to change the world and pursue that path.

PART 2

DURING THE WAIT

TIP 8 - WAIT CONSTRUCTIVELY
Talk to Admissions Officers at Each Institution Your Student Is Thinking of Attending to Determine How Admissions Decisions Are Made

DURING THE WAIT

On your tour or at another designated time, be sure to stop into the admissions office to speak with a professional about how admissions decisions are made at the institution of interest. When you are visiting, ask for the business card of the professional with whom you are speaking. Stay in contact with this person throughout your search. You will find it is a much easier process when dealing with the same person as your student makes a choice of which institution to attend. Specifically find out the application process of the schools your student is interested in attending. For most universities, admissions decisions are made based on a student's grade-point average, class rank, standardized test scores, strength of essay, strength of letters of recommendations and adherence to deadline dates.

Students, if you have not yet reached your senior year, take advantage of every opportunity you can to receive advanced tutoring, and engage yourself in activities that can bolster your academic profile. Take honors, Advanced Placement (AP) classes or work toward an International Baccalaureate (IB) diploma if you can. Stretch yourself! If you have any weak areas, seek help from your teachers or other students who excel in the area in which you are deficient. Be aware of your grades starting early in your high school career. Participate in outside activities that will expand your knowledge and allow you to grow and thrive. Remember that your grades will affect your GPA, class rank and senior standing. Once you are in your senior year of high school, do not give in to senioritis! Senioritis is real and has been going on since the beginning of time. As you approach the end of your high school career, focus on keeping your grades up and finishing strong rather than giving in and doing nothing. Stay focused until the very end of your high school career. Join meaningful organizations during your entire high school career. Complete community service activities and keep track of any special awards and honors that you receive throughout high school. Colleges like to see all of the above on applications. Try to determine which activities will set you apart from other applicants in a positive way. Lastly, some colleges honor legacy admits. Special consideration could possibly be granted if an applicant's mother or father attended the college.

TIP 9 - UNDERSTAND FINANCES
Narrow College Search and Determine Cost of Attendance (COA) at Top Choices

FINANCIAL AID

Be sure to include direct costs such as tuition, fees, housing and dining as well as indirect costs, such as books, supplies and transportation when estimating the cost of attendance. The example below reflects the COA after financial aid is factored in. You will have to calculate the COA before and after financial aid in order to make an informed decision about a particular institution.

ESTIMATED COST OF ATTENDANCE			$38,400
Tuition and fees:			$24,500
Room and board:			$9,400
Books, materials and supplies:			$1,000
Personal, travel, miscellaneous:			$2,000
Computer:			$1,500
Aid Description	**Fall**	**Spring**	**Total**
Federal Perkins Loan	$1,000	$1,000	$2,000
Federal Stafford Loan 1	$1,750	$1,750	$3,500
Federal Stafford Loan 2	$1,000	$1,000	$2,000
School Scholarship	$7,500	$7,500	$15,000
Federal Pell Grant	$500	$500	$1,000
State Scholarship	$450	$450	$900
Federal Work-Study (FWS)	$1,500	$1,500	$3,000
TOTAL AID			$27,400

TIP 10 - RESEARCH AND APPLY FOR SCHOLARSHIPS
Research General Scholarships and Specific Pools of Money

Scholarships can be awarded based upon academic merit, field of study, participation in a group or a specific membership, talent in a particular area, as well as many other specified criteria. The Internet and your local library are great resources for finding general and specific scholarships available for your student.

Perform a Google search on finding scholarships, and go to the library to research other ways to find money for college. Ask for help at the university financial aid office, diversity and inclusion office and at the college (school/department) in which your student is interested. Additionally, ask your student to check with their school counselor for help. Check out the book titled *101 Scholarship Applications: What It Takes to Obtain A Debt-Free College Education* by Gwen Richardson. Richardson through research, hard work and ingenuity, worked alongside her daughter to secure a debt-free education from an out-of-state school. The book, containing a wealth of scholarship information is updated each year and can help guide your scholarship search.

FILL OUT THE FAFSA®

The Free Application for Federal Student Aid (FAFSA®) is used to determine your student's eligibility for Federal Student Aid, which is aid available through the U.S. Department of Education to help students pay for college. Since many scholarships consider financial need as well as merit, start the process at: https://studentaid. ed.gov/sa/fafsa. Use the FAFSA® form to apply for financial aid (grants, work-study and loans) to pay for college or career school.

Students seeking financial aid are encouraged to begin the process early. Follow these steps to get started:

Step 1   Apply for a Federal Student Aid ID. Create your ID on fsaid.ed.gov.
                Both students and parents need to create their own FSA ID.
                Write this information down in the back of this book; you will
                need it from year to year as you apply for aid.

Step 2   Using your Federal Student Aid ID, go to the FAFSA® website at
                fafsa.gov and submit your application as soon as you can.

FSA ID

Social Security Number/Alien Registration Number *(non US citizens)*

Federal Tax Return/W-2, Financial Records *(students and parents)*

Bank Statements, Investments Records *(if applicable)*

Untaxed Income Records *(if applicable)*

Title IV Institution Codes for Each School Year Student Applying to *(codes can be found by searching "FAFSA federal school code search")*

FAFSA® filing opens each year on October 1. Be prepared to fill it out completely between the opening date of October 1 and November. FAFSA® information should be received by the institutions that you are considering by their specific filing deadline dates. Filing deadlines vary from school to school. It is important to file early in order to be in the pool for monies available at the institutions your student has selected. The electronic FAFSA® can accept up to 10 different schools. This means that your information, once filed, can be sent to up to 10 schools.

KEEP TRACK OF IMPORTANT INFORMATION

Once your student has applied to a college and your FAFSA® information is dispensed to the institutions that your student has chosen, mail from the institutions will begin rolling in. Be certain to establish a filing system so the mail from each university is organized and you are able to keep track of college admissions decisions, institution filing dates, specific details, and possible award letters. You can easily set up a simple filing system by obtaining an 8 1/2 by 14 mailing envelope for each institution to which your student has applied. Write the name of the institution of interest on a single envelope. Whenever you receive mail of any sort from a specific institution, put the mail into the appropriately marked envelope. You can then easily locate and read over the correspondence, which will include important dates, admission decisions, award letters, etc., and keep them safely in one place. You might want to record important dates on the outside of each institution's envelope for easy reference. Whether you use the envelope method or another one, the important thing is to keep all the correspondence together and organized so that your student is able to remain on top of things and does not miss out on anything because of disorganization. It is a good idea to reach out to any school that sends a financial aid award letter and personally speak to a financial aid counselor who will be able to walk you through the offer. Often, a financial aid award letter can seem straightforward and later needs to be clarified because expectations on the part of the receiver can seem different based upon disbursement of funds. It is best to get ahead of this issue and to make sure the prospective student and their family has a clear and correct understanding of what is being offered along with all the details.

FASTWEB

A great resource for students is Fastweb. It is free to register, and provides the student with personalized scholarship and internship matches, college scholarship applications, financial aid tips and part-time job information. Familiarize yourself with this important website. It contains so much helpful information for students throughout their college career. To get started follow the directions below:

HOW TO USE FASTWEB
Go to www.fastweb.com **Complete the profile and remember to update it on a regular basis** **Download the free College Scholarship app to get any matches generated** **Check your app to determine scholarship opportunities** **Check your email often** *(scholarships, internships, part-time job opportunities)*

Use the **WORKING PAPERS** portion of this book to keep a record of the name of scholarships you are interested in, deadline date for application, requirements, type of award, amount of award, date of application, and any follow up information pertaining to the award that you receive. Review the Federal Student Aid guide in the **SPECIAL GIFT** resources to understand additional scholarship opportunities. To find even more helpful publications, fact sheets and tools from the Office of Federal Student Aid to assist you in preparing and paying for school, go to https://studentaid.gov/resources.

When it was time for our oldest son to go to college, my husband and I were both employed in great jobs, had invested in some stocks

that were doing pretty well, and mistakenly did not fill out the FAFSA® at all. We did not know much about the process and did not have a book such as this one providing us with tips for parents of first-time college students. Even though my husband and I had attended college and obtained several degrees, when the time arose for my son to attend college, we thought we knew best. *Wrong.* Long story short, because we were both employed and we did not feel as if we met the criteria for need, we chose not to fill out the FAFSA®. News Flash: Not filling out the FAFSA® is a guarantee that you will not receive any federal aid. You will not even be in the running for it. Therefore, my son received no aid of any type for the first year of his college career.

Meanwhile, I became employed at the university my son attended during his first year of study and was working in the same college that offered his major. I worked with students who received scholarships and grants and those who did not receive aid. Then the unexpected happened: The economy took a hit we were not expecting. We could not use our investment income, so we paid out of pocket for his first year, but quickly got on board with the FAFSA® and FASTWEB for years two through four. Because of the experience with my son, we did not make the same mistake ever again. When my son was a junior, my oldest daughter was starting her first year with two other siblings starting in her third and fourth year, respectively. We made sure to fill out the FAFSA® for both of them and continued to do so for all of our children. Because of the FAFSA® our students received some grants and some loans. My youngest daughter received a full-ride academic scholarship from the university that she attended, which was wonderful; therefore, her story is different. I wish I had been privy to the advice I am giving you now back then. Please remember this if nothing else: Fill out the FAFSA®, research scholarships, complete FASTWEB, take advantage of any and all outlets, books, tips and financial aid advice that you can and do it as early as you possibly can. It really does matter!

TIP 11 - ESTIMATE FAMILY FINANCIAL SUPPORT
Assess Financial Strategy

DETERMINE HOW MUCH YOUR FAMILY WILL BE ABLE TO CONTRIBUTE (EFC)

The expected family contribution (EFC) is a measure of the family's financial strength, based on the assets and income of the parents and the prospective student. For independent students, it is also based on the income and assets of the student's spouse, if any. The EFC is also based on family size and the number of children in college. The EFC does not consider certain forms of unsecured consumer debt such as credit cards and auto loans. There are two main formulas for calculating an EFC: the federal methodology (FM) and the institutional methodology (IM). The two formulas differ in the types of assets that are considered (e.g., family home, assets of siblings), the assumption of a minimum student contribution, the treatment of paper losses, regional differences in cost of living allowances for educational savings and emergency funds, the treatment of children of divorced parents and adjustments for more than one child in college at the same time. The FM EFC is used for determining eligibility for federal and state aid and financial aid at most colleges. About 250 colleges use the IM EFC instead for awarding their own financial aid funds (fastweb.com, 2019).

CONSIDER WHETHER YOU WANT YOUR STUDENT TO WORK

If you find that your student will need to work during their college experience to help with the cost of attendance, proceed with caution. If at all possible, allow your student to forego working until they have at least experienced one full semester of study. This is important because your student will have no idea of the rigor of college coursework and will really need time to acclimate to their surroundings before taking on even a part-time job. They will need to establish a calendar and be able to manage their time and responsibilities when starting out to be able to successfully set their GPA and establish themselves as a solid student. If you have no other options and your student must work, ask them to work very limited hours at the beginning of their college career so that they can balance coursework and their job effectively. College must be their first job. If it is necessary for your student to work, they may be eligible for the work study program on their campus. Federal Work Study (FWS) is a program that is federally funded and is considered as part of the financial aid package of students who are deemed eligible. Students must file a FAFSA® as part of the application process for Federal Work Study assistance. Students who are employed in an FWS program are limited to working a specific number of hours per week, usually 10. If students are not offered a work study option, they might consider working off campus or on campus at a job that is not designated as work study, but they should limit their hours on their own until they are confident that they can handle the rigor of school along with a part-time job.

CAREFULLY CONSIDER RISK FACTORS BEFORE TAKING OUT LOANS

At one point, we had three of our four children in college at one time. I also decided to go back to school for my doctorate when my oldest son was in undergrad. Needless to say, it was not easy financially for our family during this span of years. We appreciated all of the aid we got, whether it was in the form of grants or loans. But remember, loans must be repaid even though some students with specific majors can be forgiven if certain employment criteria are met after graduation. The point that I want to make with this story is the importance of being serious about college and your studies, because if you find yourself enrolled in college and you are not serious or mature enough for this step in your life and have taken out loans, you will still have to repay them. Unfortunately, this is a hard lesson to learn-especially after the fact. This is exactly what happened in the case of our youngest son. In truth, college is not for everyone. We found this out after two wasted years and after the loans had been taken out by us as the parents and my son as the prospective student. Looking back, I now realize that even though my son said he wanted to go to college, his actions of not going to class, not studying and not striving academically proved otherwise. We have repaid our loan, but my son is still working on paying his with absolutely nothing to show for it. It is my hope that your student really desires a college education and that they are willing to work hard to obtain it. Your student will have to be intentional in their efforts to succeed. They will need to master self-management! A positive attitude and the proper mindset go a long way. If your student is ready for this next step in their lives, they will be fine. A higher education is attainable for those who desire it wholeheartedly. It is also worth the effort for any student who is willing to put in the work to obtain their degree.

PART 3
AFTER ACCEPTANCE

Once upon a time, there was a little girl in elementary school. When she was in the second grade, she had a teacher named Mr. Barucky. On a progress report that he sent home while she was in his class, he stated, "Phylicia is having some trouble with math. She's not failing but seems to have a hard time understanding some of the concepts." As a concerned parent I discussed the progress report with Phylicia and found that she "hated math" and felt she wasn't any good at it. This same message was repeated from various teachers and from Phylicia over the years as she progressed through elementary, middle, high school and eventually college.

While she never failed math, she absolutely hated it and believed that she would truly fall flat on her face in college after scoring dismally on the math portion of the ACT. At Ohio University, Phylicia was initially an elementary education major. Because of her love for children, she wanted to teach preschoolers, kindergarten or first grade. In order to be an educator, you have to pass several Praxis exams. Because of Phyl's low ACT score, she was not exempted from the Praxis exam like other students who did well on the ACT. This meant that she would have to pass both the Praxis 1 and the Praxis 2 exams to continue in the major. In the meantime, Phyl signed up for the first math class that she was required to take as an education major. She was petrified. After the first class, she showed me the syllabus and read what it contained to me over the phone. It scared me! The class was extremely strenuous, and the syllabus stated that a certain percentage had to be maintained on all tests and quizzes and that if the student fell below the specified percentage at any point during the quarter, they would fail the course. I was worried for her, but I tried to encourage her and suggested that she find her advocates. She needed to obtain a tutor, go to the math lab and stay in communication with her professor throughout the quarter. I tried to help her secure a tutor, as the first tutor that she talked to kept standing her up. I emailed a student that I knew was an education major who was a year ahead of her. He agreed to tutor her but later gave me some excuse regarding why he could not do it.

Meanwhile the tests and quizzes kept on coming. Even though she was trying and had spoken with her professor, she decided to drop the class. She "withdrew-passing" from the class. She was very discouraged and began to wonder if she would ever realize her dream of being a teacher.

When talking to her faculty advisor a few weeks later, she had a disagreement and eventually ended up changing majors altogether. However, she still wanted to work with children and hopefully teach them. In looking for a new major, Phyl dug out the college catalog and found a similar major that was offered through the College of Health and Human Services. The major was Family Studies, and a person with this major could do a great deal to help children, families and the elderly. There was also an elementary education major in this College. She was excited that she could pursue a new major and still possibly work with children.

In her new major, Phyl needed to take PSY 120: Statistics. She was still afraid of the idea of taking math (or math-related) subjects because of the negative script that she had been fed since the age of 7. She actually cried when she had to register for the class, but she did. She secured a tutor and also asked a girl in her class to study with her. She initiated all of the phone calls between the classmate and herself. In addition, she came to all the study sessions that the professor offered, went to the professor's office hours and got an A in the class! This was a real boost to her self-esteem. Phyl was beyond excited that she not only passed the class but had received an A. While she never really struggled otherwise at OU, I think receiving this grade shifted her mindset from a negative to a positive one. Phylicia really did well at OU. She never failed a class, never was on academic probation, never in trouble at all. She went from being a scared student to being a triumphant one. She graduated in four years from the College of Health and Human Services with a 3.4 GPA. I am so proud of my daughter. She started her first job a few weeks after graduation at a childcare facility in Athens, Ohio, as a preschool teacher. She currently is an Early Childhood Education Coach, in which she oversees 66 teachers over a five-state region to ensure that they are providing quality education to their preschool-aged students.

I have shared this story with students in several of the first-year seminar classes I have taught. It shows the importance of finding and utilizing your resources and advocates, and how doing so can lead to stellar results.

TIP 12 - FIND YOUR ADVOCATES

IDENTIFY STUDENT RESOURCES ON EACH CAMPUS OF INTEREST
Locate student development/student affairs offices and talk to the professionals you find working. Be sure to check out offices that can be useful to you during your stay on campus. Ideas of places to consider visiting are listed below:

Accessibility Services	Math Lab
Career Services	Multicultural Student Services
Computer Lab	Ombudsman
Counseling Services	Reading Lab
Disability Services	Residence Life
Diversity and Inclusion	Student Advising
First Year Experience	Student Retention
Greek Life	Study Tables
Health Services	Transfer Student Services
Institutional Equity	Tutoring Services
International Students	Women's Center
LGBTQ Department	Writing Lab

While the list provided above is not all inclusive, it does provide a glimpse of the many departments that can possibly be available on a particular college campus to support the students that attend there. Brief descriptions of these support offices can be found in the list that follows:

■ ACCESSIBILITY SERVICES

This office works with students who have documented disabilities to ensure access and support at a higher education institution (may also be referred to as Disability Services). Students must self-identify, have a documented disability or suspect that they have a disability that could possibly interfere with their academic performance if they wish to receive services (accommodations). Coordinators review student documents and determine eligibility according to the framework of the Americans with Disabilities Act Amendment Act. Typically, services and accommodations are provided for students with:

Learning disabilities	Hearing impairments/deafness
ADD/ADHD	Mobility impairments
Psychological conditions	Visual impairments/blindness
Chronic illnesses	Other disabilities

CAREER SERVICES
works with students to provide guidance in choosing a major, exploring career options and securing internships or employment upon graduation

COMPUTER LAB
provides computers for student use on campus for students who need computer access

COUNSELING AND PSYCHOLOGICAL SERVICES
provides mental health and psychological services to students, faculty and staff

DISABILITY SERVICES
see Accessibility Services

DIVERSITY AND INCLUSION
seeks to facilitate that an infusion of diversity is embedded into the lives and experiences of the students enrolled in an institution of higher education

GREEK LIFE
assists the fraternity and sorority community on campus in reaching their specific chapter goals and initiatives

HEALTH SERVICES
a health and wellness resource for students and staff of a university

INSTITUTIONAL EQUITY
protects students against discrimination, harassment and sexual violence, and ensures that the university is in compliance with federal and state laws

■ INTERNATIONAL STUDENTS
provides support to students from other countries who are studying in the US

■ LEARNING COMMUNITIES DEPARTMENT
manages students who belong to a particular learning community to ensure that the cohort is successful in a specific course through collaboration and accountability

■ LGBTQ DEPARTMENT
provides support and a safe, inclusive and equitable environment for students, faculty and staff who identify as lesbian, gay, bisexual, transgender or queer

■ MATH LAB
offers free tutorial help to students enrolled in any math-related courses such as accounting, statistics, economics or math

■ MULTICULTURAL STUDENT SERVICES
provides support, and promotes inclusion and engagement for students who are underrepresented at an institution

■ OFFICE OF THE OMBUDS (OMBUDSMAN)
a confidential service that is open to all students to help deal with equitable and fair treatment and due process and to provide support and facilitate a fair learning and working environment

■ READING LAB
facilitates student efforts to improve reading skills, think critically and communicate more effectively

■ RESIDENCE LIFE
provides housing, support services and programming for on-campus students

■ STUDENT ADVISING
assists with choosing majors, selecting courses, and satisfying degree requirements

▨ STUDENT RETENTION

assists students in identifying and incorporating strategies for success relative to academic persistence at an institution for higher education

▨ STUDY TABLES

provides a quiet place for groups and individual students to study, often arranged for students who participate in sports or those in particular scholarship groups or learning communities

▨ TRANSFER STUDENT SERVICES

works with students who desire to transfer their enrollment and credits from one institution to another

▨ TUTORING SERVICES

provides academic support for students who are experiencing academic difficulty

▨ WOMEN'S CENTER

supports the professional growth of women and gender minorities by promoting justice and fostering connections on campus

▨ WRITING LAB

facilitates student efforts to improve their writing skills, critical thinking and communication skills

▨ VETERANS SERVICES

supports students as they make the transition from military duty to campus life

TIP 13 - CHOOSE YOUR ROOMMATE

As a first-year student you may find that it is required for you to stay on campus at most residential universities. You will want to decide whether you would prefer to live in a single room, double room, or perhaps a quad. If you would like a roommate, you will need to decide the best way of going about finding that person. But before picking a roommate you should know yourself. What kind of person are you? Do you have any habits that may be offensive to others? Are you a social person or more of a loner? Do you prefer to study in a quiet place or do you prefer background noise? Are you messy or clean? Have you ever had to share a room? These are just a few of the questions you should answer before you begin searching for a roommate.

If you are attending college with your best friend you might think it is a good idea to room together. It might be, but please realize that there is a big difference between being great friends and being able to live together. You might want to rethink this particular choice because it can be very hard to room with friends on campus, typically due to too much familiarity. Friends who become roommates also might begin to take advantage of the friendship and not take as much care as they need to show respect for the property and personal spaces of one another. If this is the case, it might be better to have a randomly assigned roommate or a matched roommate. Some universities utilize a software program which has incoming first-year students fill out a questionnaire and then uses the answers to match roommate pairs. The questions are designed to find areas of commonality between students in an attempt to match like-minded students with one another. After a match is generated students are made aware of their matches and have the option of reaching out to them before move-in day. At that time each party can decide if it looks like they can establish rapport and formulate ground rules before committing to the other. If you have an open mind and are willing to take a chance, you might actually find a life-long friend and will get to know a great person whom you might have never had the opportunity to meet.

Additionally, you can also choose to be housed in a learning community with a group of your peers or can be randomly assigned. Regardless of the way in which you obtain a roommate you should remember that you will spend a great deal of time in your room and the room should be a place where all parties are comfortable and feel at ease. Establishing ground rules with your roommate whether they are a friend, acquaintance or a previously unknown person is especially important. Regardless of who you room with things like bed times, study times, respect for the property of one another, room guests, and use of common areas in the room should be discussed. Once both parties can agree on the setup and ground rules it's much easier to co-exist and find fit in your new home away from home.

TIP 14 - ORGANIZE YOURSELF

TIME MANAGEMENT

There are 168 hours in a week. As a responsible college student, you must use every bit of your time wisely. A great way to stay on task is to utilize a calendar, planner or your phone to organize yourself to be able to keep your commitments, take care of coursework, study and

" ESTABLISH A DAILY TO DO LIST "

plan recreation time. Start with a calendar. It is much easier to see everything on your schedule all at once and to be able to plan your days effectively. While in college you should be prepared to spend approximately two to three hours studying for each hour spent in class. So, if you spend two hours in a particular class, you should spend four to six hours studying that specific subject. If you are having difficulty in a particular class, you may need to allocate more time during the week for study. If you are registered as a full-time college student (taking 12 credit hours), you will need to allocate 24 to 36 hours per week. To manage your time properly you will need to take an assessment on how you spend your time initially, and then make a conscious effort to eliminate time wasters. You will need to plan your days.

8 REASONS TO PLAN
1   To Make Things Happen
2   To Get Further in Your Career (right now your career is "college student")
3   To Make Better Decisions
4   To Take Control of Your Time and Ultimately Your Life
5   To Give Direction to Energy
6   To Gain Confidence
7   To Increase Self-Esteem
8   To Achieve Your Goals

Use a planner or an Excel spreadsheet based upon the sample sheets included in the **WORKING PAPERS** section to keep track of your activities. You should establish a daily "to do" list. Each page should include the following sections: Task List, Priority Number, Date and Notes, along with a daily planning worksheet.

DAILY TIME MANAGEMENT VS. OVERALL TIME MANAGEMENT

It is helpful to think of time management as two intersecting layers. Overall time management involves reviewing long term goals, setting priorities and making plans to meet those goals. Daily time management includes activities that will help you organize your time and resources to meet your larger goals. Your larger goal will be graduating from your university.

■ TO ACHIEVE OVERALL TIME MANAGEMENT

Review your career goals

Establish long- and short-range objectives

Make a list of long-term, monthly and weekly objectives; prioritize your list

Build a support network

Eliminate time wasters

Take scheduled breaks

Be consistent

■ TO ACHIEVE DAILY TIME MANAGEMENT

Make daily "to do" lists and assign them priority numbers

Review lists daily to eliminate or reassign priority numbers assigned to tasks

Do one job at a time

Plan every minute

Assign yourself some time for relaxation

Learn to say no

Use a calendar initially to see the big picture

Be consistent

There are many ways to become and remain organized by controlling your time. Depending on the strategy that works best for you, set up a method to ensure that you stay on top of your responsibilities. You can set up a calendar or planner using an Excel spreadsheet, or you might want to use a calendar app on your phone if you feel that will work better for you. If you would like to use a time management, calendar or planner app on your phone, browse the internet for apps that are easy to download to your phone and easy to use. There are a variety of types of calendar apps available online for download. Google "calendar apps for phones" to check out what is available. Regardless of the method you choose to become organized, choose one or several to stay on top of the many activities that you will certainly face as a college student.

TIP 15 - INCORPORATE PERSONAL BUDGETING

In order to become financially responsible as a college student, it is necessary to have a handle on your personal finances. In order to effectively gain control of your finances, you should know exactly how much money is coming in and how much money is going out of your personal accounts. Making the most of your money while in college can be challenging. As a first-year student, you may find that you must work at least part-time in order to meet the financial challenges that you might face. Although it is not recommended that you work more than a few hours (if at all, especially during the first year), many students find that they simply have to do so. Regardless of whether you work, you will need to establish a personal budget to stay on top of your finances. Personal budgeting is about tracking your monthly income and expenses to ensure that your expenses stay within your limits. An easy method to utilize when establishing a personal budget is to create an Excel spreadsheet to track your income and expenses over an entire school year. You may use the sheet located in the **WORKING PAPERS** portion of this book as a guide for creating your own personal Excel chart.

DETERMINE INCOME

Determining your income sounds easy, however there are many ways in which monthly income can fluctuate over the course of a school year. Start by first making a list of all sources of income and take the following categories into consideration:

+ **EMPLOYMENT INCOME**
  money from your job if you are working

+ **ALLOWANCE**
  monies received from family and friends

+ **GIFTS**
  any monies received as gifts

+ **REFUNDS AND REIMBURSEMENTS**
  tax refund income, or any reimbursements received

DETERMINE EXPENSES

Much like sources of income, monthly expenditures also can fluctuate. Start by making a list of all expenses, while taking the following categories into consideration:

− **FIXED EXPENSES**
  bills that have the same amount due from month to month

− **VARIABLE EXPENSES**
  bills that have a varied amount due from month to month

− **DISCRETIONARY EXPENSES**
  the purchase of items that are not necessary for survival

Using your fixed expenses such as cell phone charges, supplies, credit card bill and other bills, prepare your budget. Your net income will be the result of subtracting your total expenses from your total income. By properly budgeting you will know exactly where your money is being spent. If you find that you are spending too much at any given time and your expenses exceed your income, you can make changes by eliminating some of your discretionary expenses, or you can focus on reducing some of your variable expenses to bring your budget into balance. Establishing and sticking to a personal budget will help you develop life skills that you will be able to use forever. Starting now to live within your budget will help you to be in a better position financially after graduation.

ECONOMICAL TIPS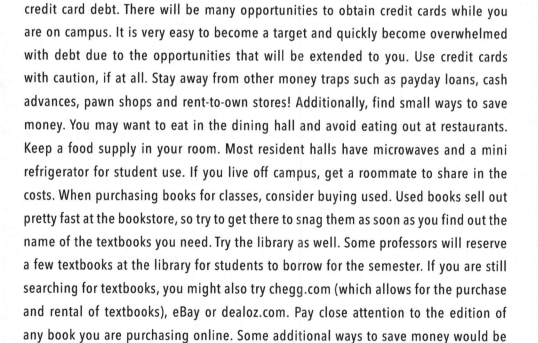

Don't be tempted to fall into the trap that is set for first-year college students regarding credit card debt. There will be many opportunities to obtain credit cards while you are on campus. It is very easy to become a target and quickly become overwhelmed with debt due to the opportunities that will be extended to you. Use credit cards with caution, if at all. Stay away from other money traps such as payday loans, cash advances, pawn shops and rent-to-own stores! Additionally, find small ways to save money. You may want to eat in the dining hall and avoid eating out at restaurants. Keep a food supply in your room. Most resident halls have microwaves and a mini refrigerator for student use. If you live off campus, get a roommate to share in the costs. When purchasing books for classes, consider buying used. Used books sell out pretty fast at the bookstore, so try to get there to snag them as soon as you find out the name of the textbooks you need. Try the library as well. Some professors will reserve a few textbooks at the library for students to borrow for the semester. If you are still searching for textbooks, you might also try chegg.com (which allows for the purchase and rental of textbooks), eBay or dealoz.com. Pay close attention to the edition of any book you are purchasing online. Some additional ways to save money would be to shop sales and ask for discounts when you can. Go to thrift or consignment stores, use coupons, shop with a friend to take advantage of buying in bulk or two-for-one deals, buy generic brands, sell excess stuff on eBay, Poshmark, Facebook Marketplace or other sites, and always be on the lookout for new ways to save.

TIP 16 - START STRONG ACADEMICALLY

ACADEMIC ADVISING

Take advantage of academic advising. Good advising may be the single most underestimated characteristic of a successful college experience. Graduating seniors state that certain kinds of advising were critical for their success (Light, 2001). Your institution likely employs paid academic advisors who are  ready and willing to help you with a myriad of things, including how to set your class schedules. Academic advisors may be busy, but it is imperative to your success that you utilize the information that they are able to provide you. You will find that you will need to become aware of prerequisites, add and drop deadlines, and many other things that can easily be overwhelming. Your advisor will be able to help you along the way. Use of academic advisors will help you immensely, especially at the beginning of your college career when you are just learning the ropes.

Students arriving at college immediately confront a myriad of decisions: which major to choose, what activities to join, how to study, where to live, how to seek help, etc. Often these decisions are made with limited information, yet their consequences can be enormous. A subject that is bypassed or study habits that are not sufficient for the associated classes can result in limited options, reduced opportunities or closed doors. Advisors play a critical role (Light, 2001). Make sure to take advantage of them.

SCHEDULE CLASSES WISELY

Do not overload yourself with too many credits or rigorous courses at the same time. This is a recipe for disaster. Be aware of prerequisites. If you miss taking a prerequisite class, you may be held up in completing your coursework in a timely manner. Be aware of required courses that are offered only once a year. If you miss taking the course in the proper semester, you will have to wait until the following academic year to complete it. As a first-year student you may be registering last for your classes since registration is often based upon credit hours successfully completed. Prepare several tentative schedules of classes each semester and discuss the possibilities of each scenario with your advisor since you may not always be able to get your first choice of schedule because of full classes, late registration time or lack of prerequisites. Improper scheduling will most likely result in extra semesters in college.

Also make wise choices when preparing your schedule regarding when your classes are held. Determine if you are a morning person. If you are not, you might not want to schedule classes at 8:00 am on a Monday. Try to schedule classes so that you are not taking too many classes with labs or more than two required classes in your major during the same semester. Include some general education requirement classes or electives for a better, less stressful experience if possible. Ask for help from your advisor and your professors in order to make the best use of your time.

NAVIGATE THE CULTURE

There is a culture everywhere. On a job there is a culture. In college there is a culture. As a first-year student you must understand the culture in which you now find yourself. Each classroom also has a culture. It is your job to adapt to that culture. Each professor has a specific way of teaching and managing their classroom. To be successful as a student, you will need to find out the specific benchmarks of navigating each classroom's culture, meet those benchmarks and then exceed those benchmarks. In other words, find out specifically what your professor expects in the classroom, then meet and exceed those expectations.

DETERMINE YOUR LEARNING STYLES

Information enters your brain in three main ways: sight, hearing and touch. The one that you use the most is called your learning style. Visual learners learn by sight and prefer to see information depicted as pictures, graphs, diagrams, cartoons and demonstrations. They picture words and concepts as images in their heads. Because of this, they are easily distracted in lecture classes when there are no visual aids. Visual learners benefit from charts, maps, notes and flashcards when studying. Auditory learners learn by hearing information spoken. They can absorb lecture information without much effort at all and may not need to take careful notes in order to learn. Auditory learners may benefit from reading aloud to themselves or using music while studying. Kinesthetic learners learn by touch and prefer touch as their primary mode for learning. In traditional lecture classes, they should write out important facts and should create study sheets that include memorable examples. Role playing can also be used in order to help with information retention. To find out what your learning style is, you may want to:

■ Take an assessment to determine your learning style

■ Think about your past favorite classes. What do they have in common?

■ Determine if you prefer: mastering facts, discussions, working in groups, working on your own, or hands-on activities

Knowing your learning style, along with both your strengths and weaknesses, can help you study more effectively, resulting in better information retention and higher grades. Once you have determined your learning style, make the best use of it by working harder in classes to adapt the material to the way you learn best.

SET YOUR GPA

Another way to get off to a great start for early success is to set your GPA. Getting an A or B on the first graded assignment in all of your courses should be a main priority (Blerkom, 2004). Do your absolute best to get the highest grades in your courses for the first semester. If possible, strive to get on the Dean's List. This will give you a strong start to your academic career and will demonstrate your commitment to your education to yourself and others. It is very hard to come back from an academic deficit. Start strong, assignment by assignment, and work to build a strong foundation from the beginning. Show that you are engaged in class. Ask relevant questions, take notes, show interest and ask for help. If you do poorly in a class, consider retaking it to raise your grade point average. Keep in mind also that at some universities, certain classes cannot be taken for a higher grade. These are usually developmental classes that are offered in an effort to build your academic skills, or first-year seminar classes that are not counted toward your major. Try your best in every class you take, whether it is in your major or developmental. Please note that failing and retaking classes will extend your time in college.

> ## TRY YOUR BEST IN EVERY CLASS

GET TO KNOW YOUR PROFESSORS

Communicate with your professors. Professors are people, too. They want to get to know you and to interact with you. Frequent and rewarding informal contact with faculty members is a strong predictor of student success and persistence to complete a degree. Additionally, studies show that ongoing contact outside of class also provides strong motivation for students to perform well inside the classroom (Davis, 2009). When communicating with your professor whether in person or by email, be sure to use proper etiquette. Professors with doctorate degrees should be addressed with the prefix "Dr." at each occurrence. Do not address any professor by their first name unless they have given you permission to do so. Follow the same rules when sending email or text messages to your professors. Remember you will need your professors in the future for letters of recommendation and they will not be able to speak up for you if they do not know you. Respect their time and craft. Take advantage of your professors' office hours to meet them and discuss any issues you may have throughout the semester. If you are experiencing difficulty at any time, meet with your professor. Do not wait until the last minute to discuss issues or problems you are having with the coursework. Professors will be more apt to help someone who they see is putting forth effort. Most professors will help you by critiquing your work and letting you know if you are on the right track. Develop a relationship with your professors–their knowledge and wisdom can be of great benefit to you while you are on campus and after graduation. Be an informed and "present" student. Sit in the front of the class and attend class regularly. A student who sits in the back of the classroom is often viewed by the professor as an unengaged, uncommitted student. Remember each professor is different. Their courses are very important to them. Once again, determine what their specific goals and expectations are for you as a student and then do everything in your power to meet and then exceed them.

Do not throw away your syllabi; they are given out for a purpose. The class syllabus is basically an overview of what will be happening in the course with which it is associated. The syllabus is so important that most professors spend the first day of class reviewing it. However, after the first day, it is your responsibility as a student to keep track of the information outlined on the syllabus. Your syllabi contain valuable information to help you be successful in class (due dates, quiz and test dates, assignments, class and attendance policies). Remember you are primarily on your own and responsible for keeping track of your time and assignments. Use of a planner will be especially helpful to keep you on top of everything.

Participate in class whether you are getting a participation grade or not. Turn in project work early (before the due date) for review if possible.

ESTABLISH YOUR NETWORK

Set a goal to get to know one faculty member well per semester. Also have that faculty member get to know you reasonably well. If you complete this task, over the course of eight semesters, you will have gotten to know eight professors. These professors can serve as references for jobs and can help when you need  letters of recommendation for graduate or professional school, jobs or fellowships after college. Students who have taken this advice state that it was the single most helpful suggestion they received during their first year of college (Light, 2001).

ADJUST TO LEARNING ONLINE

Most recently, online education has come to the forefront as never before in the history of higher education. As online classes are becoming more prevalent, keep in mind that you may find yourself in an online class more than once during your undergraduate career. When participating in an online class here are a few tips you should keep in mind for success.

Be present in each class. You will want to pay close attention to class interactions and take effective notes while in class. Participate in class as an effort to engage with your professor. Participating will make the experience more enjoyable for you as well as your fellow students.

Before the first class session, become familiar with the virtual classroom software tool being utilized. Log in early to class. During class, eliminate as many distractions as possible and focus on what is happening on your computer monitor. Remove any inappropriate items that are in the area that others can see behind or near you. Tell other people who are in your space that you are participating in a live class session. Ask that they be mindful of their appearance or that they stay out of the camera shot.

If you are utilizing Zoom or another platform for online classroom sessions, take advantage of the "mute" button. This will allow the classroom to be quiet enough for everyone to hear the lesson and will also minimize distractions due to noise during class. Just remember to unmute your microphone to participate in discussions, ask questions and interact with other students as necessary. Remember when interacting that your professor and other students are not able to take advantage of nonverbal communication cues as in a traditional classroom.

Learn how to send a private message to your professor in case you need to do so. If you become disconnected from the internet during the class, just log back in as quickly as you can. If you have excessive connectivity issues, discuss this with your professor.

Treat the online class seriously and be respectful of the class setting at all times. Learning in an online format may be a bit different than what you are accustomed to, but it is certainly possible to experience success in such classes. Be responsible and respectful. Set yourself up for success and you will certainly achieve it.

ADAPT TO THE UNEXPECTED

Throughout your education journey, unexpected things can and will occur that have the potential to derail you if you are not prepared to adapt. For example, in the early months of 2020, the world rapidly had to endure many changes in higher education as colleges shut down in order to prevent the spread of COVID-19. First-time students, as well as seasoned students, suddenly found themselves having to face a new reality in regards to their college experience. When unexpected things occur or plans change, you don't have to lose ground in your pursuit of higher education. Adapt to the new reality and continue to put forth your best effort. Regardless of any changes at your college or university, continue to establish yourself as a serious and solid student. Make sure to study and take your assignments seriously. Don't become distracted because you are not experiencing college as you previously expected. Use your time wisely and make the best of this time in your life. Many people are counting on you. Make them and yourselves proud! Be flexible and adaptable. A good attitude goes a long way in finding contentment in your life and reaching your dreams.

TIP 17 - STAY SAFE

As a new student on campus you may find yourself on your own for the very first time. You will need to be especially careful about your surroundings because crime on campus happens. Because of this fact, The Clery Act, named in memory of Jeanne Clery, a 19-year-old who was sexually assaulted and murdered in her college dormitory, stipulates that college campuses must have detailed emergency alert systems in place for their campus community members and that they must report crime statistics that occur on, near or in off-campus facilities (Carmichael, 2012).

To stay safe on your campus you should be diligent about the following:

- Take advantage of escorts on campus after dark or anytime you feel unsafe
- Be aware of and utilize the safety procedures your campus has in place to avoid danger
- Lock your room door at all times and store your valuables carefully to avoid theft
- Report any issues you see or suspect to your resident advisor and/or the campus police
- Tell someone when you are going out, with whom you are going, and when you expect to return
- Drop a pin of your final destination to a close friend
- Keep your cell phone charged at all times
- Be aware of your surroundings
- Travel in groups or pairs if possible
- Be aware of safety telephones on your campus
- Learn self-defense

- Watch your alcohol content

- Do not accept open drinks, especially from people you don't know

- Utilize safety apps on your phone to track your movements from point A to point B such as On watch, Guardly, or bSafe

- Leave events at the same time as the friends you arrived with

- If using headphones make sure you can still hear outside noise

TIP 18 - OBSERVE CAMPUS RULES

As an admitted student to your university, you are expected to conduct yourself responsibly both on and off-campus. Rules and standards for campus conduct are established for the safety and well-being of the university community. Therefore, you need to understand that violations of the university code of conduct and/or local laws can seriously impede your progress in achieving your degree as well as harm other members of the community. It is your responsibility as a student to familiarize yourself with the code of conduct to which you must adhere. The code of conduct can be easily found on the university website and in your application materials. A code of conduct refers to rules, regulations, and procedures and encompasses both academic and non-academic misconduct. Areas of academic misconduct include cheating, plagiarism, or any conduct that violates the trust of another in an academic setting. Non-academic misconduct violates civil or criminal laws.

There are many reasons why students should strive to abide by the laws put in place by their institutions. First of all, it's the right thing to do. Students who find themselves in trouble are distracted in the worst way from being able to gain their education, which is (or should be) the primary goal of attending college. Students found in violation of the laws of their campus community may be held responsible by the university. Punishments for violating university rules can range from a reprimand to expulsion, depending on the offense.

Often violations committed on campus or lesser issues might be reviewed by the university's office of student conduct and can result in probation, loss of scholarships and temporary suspension. Students in violation may also be subject to a disciplinary hearing held on campus. Additionally, most campuses have university police stations on-site, staffed with fully trained officers, to handle offenses that occur on campus.

When misconduct is severe or has taken place off-campus, local law enforcement personnel usually become involved to resolve the issue. Measures taken at the local level are more severe and may result in steep fines, incarceration, embarrassment, a criminal record, expulsion, and much more, not to mention the collateral damage that may occur as a result of such actions. To avoid situations of this type, follow the rules and laws of your campus and local communities. Stay far away from situations that could derail you from reaching your goal of attending college and obtaining your degree.

TIP 19 - STAY THE COURSE

IDENTIFY YOUR PERSONAL SUPPORT SYSTEM

An important part of being able to stay the course depends upon you as a student working to become and remain comfortable on the campus you have chosen. Nothing can contribute to the loneliness that most first-year students initially experience more than feeling socially isolated in the environment in which you will be living for the next four years or more. If you are a member of a special population such as African American or Hispanic student, woman, commuter student, other ability, or LGBTQ student, you may experience additional adjustment issues while at college. When searching for a college, make sure that there are efforts of inclusion of the groups that you identify with personally and other diverse students as well. Look for programs and departments that are inclusive and are designed to help students who are members of special populations. When searching for a campus, hopefully you found one that made you feel welcome, and one in which you could picture yourself growing and learning. Now it is time to engage yourself in organizations, find friends and participate in activities where you are affirmed and where you experience a feeling of belonging. Now is the time to get connected. There are many organizations you can join and choices you can make to ensure that you are not isolated during your time on campus.

Be aware that many first-year students experience feelings of homesickness because they are used to being surrounded by loved ones at home and suddenly find themselves alone in a totally new and strange environment. To combat feelings of isolation and loneliness, be sure to check out organizations and groups that you can interact with on your campus. Check out some of the following ways you can make connections in your new home.

■ CAMPUS ORGANIZATIONS

Your campus may host organization fairs that are essentially a forum where many campus-recognized organizations will set up tables to inform you about their respective organizations in an effort to persuade you to join them. These fairs are usually held at the beginning of the semester soon after you move to campus. There are also many Greek letter organizations that you might want to explore. Greek letter organizations are social and service organizations at institutions of higher education. Membership in these organizations usually occurs during your undergraduate experience and can continue for a lifetime. However, you might want to wait until after your first year to join a Greek letter organization because of the time commitment that is required in order to become a member.

■ LEARNING COMMUNITIES

Membership in a First-Year Cohort or Learning Community can also ease the transition for you as a first-year student. Typically, first-year students who are assigned to a particular major within a department or school are assigned to a cohort or learning community. The members of the group are able to experience college as a group rather than individually. The cohort usually are enrolled in several courses together and meet with a departmental advisor throughout the first year. If you are a scholarship recipient, you may already have a group of potential friends. You will be, most likely, taking classes and performing community service projects together and meeting with a program/scholarship director on a regular basis. The members of your scholarship cohort may become lifelong friends. Becoming plugged into a cohort is a great idea to alleviate the initial feeling of isolation and loneliness that first-year students typically face. However it is important to note that first-year cohorts or learning communities are often just that. They are typically set up during the first year only. It is the responsibility of the student to form friendships with others that will last beyond the first year.

◼ MENTORS

Find mentors that can help you navigate your way. You can find mentors easily by finding someone to emulate who has been on a path similar to the one that you are now on. Stay in contact with your mentors because the information that they will share with you is invaluable. Also realize that as you go through experiences, others may wish for you to mentor them. You have something to offer others as well. Learn from your experiences and then share the information with others who are coming behind you. Associating yourself with others who are in the same boat or with those who have experienced a similar path is a great goal to have. You will find that attending college and being in new surroundings will be much easier for you as a member of a group rather than solely on your own.

◼ FRIENDS

Find your friends. As mentioned before, participation in groups or organizations with like-minded students can lead to lasting friendships. Whether from participating in groups, from your classmates or from another source, your new friends will be supportive of you and you can support them in return. It is important that you develop friendships to encourage, inspire and challenge you. You in turn can do the same for them.

Keep in mind that regardless of what organizations you commit to or friend groups you develop, you must be careful not to overextend yourself. Make sure that you remain focused on your studies and your overall goals at all times.

PRACTICE SELF CARE BY MANAGING STRESS

Being healthy as a student goes a long way toward staying the course toward successfully completing a college career. It is extremely difficult to perform well academically while suffering mentally or physically. As a college student you must practice self-care against mental and physical illness. Stress is the body's automatic response to any physical or mental demand placed on it. It is the body's reaction to the events occurring in our lives. Although not all stress is bad, it's important to manage excess stress in your life so that you can effectively perform as a college student.

STRESS IS PHYSICAL

When we are under stress, our bodies react with the fight or flight response. Adrenalin and other chemicals are pumped into the bloodstream as our bodies prepare to spring into action.

STRESS IS MENTAL

Stress isn't all in your head, but that's where it starts. Events don't necessarily cause stress; how you interpret and react to them is what causes stress.

STRESS IS POWERFUL

Many people do their best work under pressure. Stress is a powerful force for growth as we often learn the most when we are forced to. Excessive stress can be harmful. Stress hurts when it becomes a way of life. The accumulated effects of long-term stress have been linked to heart disease, ulcers, and cancer.

Stress management begins with identifying the sources of stress in your life. Stressors are situations, activities, and relationships that cause pain or harm to you physically, emotionally or psychologically. For some individuals, stressors can be identified as:

School	Finances	Work
Family issues	Health/illness	Relationships
Environment	Legal issues	Disorganization

As a student, you will need to manage your stress. Once you identify your stressors, be sure to incorporate exercise, time management and relaxation into your daily schedule. Any time you find yourself becoming stressed, logically assess the situation. Take a few minutes to quiet your mind and gain perspective.

TIPS FOR COMBATTING STRESS

1. BELIEVE IN YOUR ABILITY TO HANDLE STRESS

- Embrace your strengths
- Identify the emotions you are feeling (anger, fear, happiness, sadness)
- Be responsible for your emotions
- Remind yourself that you can influence the outcome of events in your life
- Create action plans to address problems you face
- Accept and observe thoughts and feelings without fighting them
- Take action to change your circumstances

2. LEARN RELAXATION TECHNIQUES

- Try deep, slow, rhythmic breathing or take a few abdominal breaths in and out through your nose
- Do visualization and meditation practices (focus on something in your environment and allow yourself to become interested in that specific item)
- Remember a peaceful scene in which you felt calm (try to remember what you said, heard, thought, and felt)
- Do gentle stretching exercises at your desk

3. UNDERSTAND GUILT

- Recognize that guilt robs you of your focus and motivation
- Develop realistic expectations for yourself
- Understand that you are not perfect

4. TALK TO SOMEONE

Find a trustworthy friend to talk with

- Talk to an objective and relaxed person
- Call a friend for a long chat

- Let someone do you a favor

- Understand that you are important

5. DEVELOP LEISURE TIME ACTIVITIES

- Join an organization

- Play intramural sports

- Listen to some favorite songs or relaxation music

- Binge-watch a TV show

- Start a workout plan

6. ESTABLISH AN EXERCISE ROUTINE

- Try and get at least 20 minutes of aerobic exercise three times a week

- Take a walk and enjoy the fresh air

7. GET PLENTY OF REST

- If you have trouble sleeping, exercise more

- Relax each part of your body as you quietly lie in bed

- Take a warm shower or hot bath before bedtime

8. EAT A BALANCED DIET

- Include many fresh fruits and vegetables in your daily diet

- Add calcium in the form of milk, yogurt or cheese each day

- Limit processed foods

- Take essential vitamins and supplements

9. DEVELOP APPROPRIATE COMMUNICATION SKILLS

- Ask for help when you need it

- Let go of blaming and complaining

- Use humor when appropriate

- Start a journal or blog

10. LEARN TO ACCEPT AND ADAPT TO CHANGE IN YOUR LIFE

- Realize change is a fact of life
- Take time to recover, refocus, and regenerate during a major change
- Be kind to yourself
- Keep your head up and seek out your support system

MENTAL HEALTH

College students are among the highest number of people who struggle with mental illnesses. Feelings of anxiety and depression are two of the most commonly reported symptoms among college students. Up to 80% of college students report struggling with feelings of depression and hopelessness. Sources of stress for most college students that can have an effect on mental health include but are not limited to:

Academic demand	Finances	Homesickness
Post-graduate plans	Relationships	Substance abuse

Mental health struggles are manifested through depression, sleep deprivation, anxiety, eating disorders, addictions and substance abuse. Ways in which mental health symptoms can be minimized or reduced are as follows:

- Acknowledge mental health issues
- Set personal goals
- Establish daily routines
- Establish self-care routines
- Maintain open communication channels

Experiencing poor mental health is certainly problematic to your academic success. Any student experiencing mental health issues will need to identify sources of help in order to thrive in college and in daily life. Places to seek help on campus are:

- Health Center
- Psychological Services
- Support groups

PHYSICAL HEALTH

Keeping in shape physically is so important to your success as a student. Take advantage of the campus gym or fitness center. Incorporate an exercise plan and develop relaxation techniques in your daily life. You also may want to take vitamins and or essential supplements as well.

SEEK NEW EXPERIENCES

As an upper-class student, when you have a handle on your course requirements, you may want to embark upon an independent study with a professor in your college. You can make a proposal to your professor of what you would like to do for your credit hours relating to your interests and the professor's specialty. The amount of credit hours you receive for your efforts depends upon the university. The professor will review your proposal and establish various check-in dates to meet with you throughout the semester to ensure that you are fulfilling your plan, while giving you suggestions and tweaks along the way. This is a great way to conduct research in an area of interest that is not covered as much in your coursework, or to complete any major-related activity you may be interested in pursuing. Take some classes just for fun if you have extra time in your schedule. A break from the more rigorous courses associated with your major is a way to relieve stress and tension. Before you graduate, you may also want to consider studying abroad to experience life in other countries. There are study abroad offices on most university campuses.

STUDENT LIFE BALANCE

There is a feature on new cars that allows for the side mirrors to light up when other cars are in the blind spot of the person driving the car. While this is very useful and perhaps helps to alleviate accidents, in real life, accidents and unexpected occurrences can and will happen. In your life there will not be a mirror that warns you of these occurrences–they just happen–but you should be on the lookout for them on your own. Many unexpected things can happen to you while you are navigating your college experience. You will need to identify the issues as they come and deal with them one by one. Some of the issues you may face might be having to drop a class, failing a class, sickness of yourself or a loved one, broken relationships and death in the family, among other things. Some of these issues will be out of your control.

Others can be managed or better yet, prepared for. You will have to learn effective ways in which to manage the occurrences in your life that can be managed by staying on top of your game mentally and physically. Staying on top of your classes is key because, after all, you are in college for a reason. Keep that reason at the forefront of your mind. Just know that you are not alone. Life happens to everyone who is living it. Identify your support systems (advocates) and use them, do your best to stay on top of your game, and learn to look out for your blindspots and deal with them as they come on your own or with the help of your advocates.

MICROMANAGE YOUR OWN DESTINY

Little fish, big pond. As a new student who has been thrust in the transition from high school to college, you are on your way. There is a big difference between what you experienced as a high school student and what you are experiencing as a first-year college student. One thing I hope you have realized by reading this book is that you are responsible for your own destiny. You have the tools necessary to make your way and the support system is available on your campus. The thing to remember is that it is up to you to manage all these aspects of your college career. You must manage your time, you must go to classes, you must study, you must manage your personal accounts, you must utilize your support system. You must undertake all aspects of your college existence. If you need special accommodations, you must request services through your university's disability service office even though professors are directed to include information in their class syllabi and to verbally instruct their students about services and accommodations in each initial class session (Davis, 2009). You are in charge of your own life and your own destiny, perhaps for the very first time.

You may feel like a little fish in a big pond and like a fish out of water. Your life and future are yours for the shaping. Take charge of your own destiny. Ready, set, sink or swim!

PREPARE FOR GRADUATION AND YOUR FUTURE

As you progress from year to year at your university, you will find that it will soon be time for graduation. As the time approaches, you will need to begin to think about your future outside of college. Throughout your college experience, be on the lookout for opportunities to intern at companies of interest. Many colleges have offices that are dedicated to helping students secure internship experiences. Continue to meet with your advisor if necessary for next steps. Your professors can also be useful in helping you to become introduced to individuals who can help you in seeking future employment.

Pay close attention to deadlines for registering (applying) for graduation and stay on top of your studies. As you near the finish line, do not fall into a slump; you are almost there. Pay more than one visit to career services. This office will be invaluable to you as you begin searching for a position. Set yourself up with organizations that can help you in your future. There are many resources that are still available to you. You can often work with your university's career services department beyond graduation.

Interested in starting your own business? Obtain a SCORE mentor who has been working in your field of interest. SCORE is the nation's largest network of volunteer, expert business mentors, with a mission to help small businesses succeed. Take advantage of the advice, webinars and courses these seasoned mentors provide for free in your area of interest. Go to score.org for more information.

You may want to continue your education and pursue a graduate degree or attend law or medical school. If so, you will need to take the necessary steps to do so. If you have not visited your university's graduate services department, you should do so to find out next steps and requirements necessary for admission to graduate school. If you plan to attend graduate school elsewhere, you will need to find out the requirements.

TIP 20 - BECOME A LIFELONG LEARNER

A life-long learner is someone who is constantly learning personally or in their professional lives. As you pursue your college degree keep in mind that you are never too old to learn. Always crave knowledge. It is one thing you can't have too much of. Expand your horizons over the course of your college years and beyond. Endeavor to learn as much as you can and don't forget to take full advantage of the opportunities available to you. As time permits, get involved in clubs, study abroad, engage with people from other cultures, sign up for electives that are interesting to you. Ask questions of others. Never stop moving forward. Learn and grow from your mistakes. Begin reading beyond your coursework for pleasure. Develop your own critical thinking skills to be able to problem solve. Seek resources to learn independently such as LinkedIn Learning and take advantage of tutorials and short courses available online. Develop your research skills. Take advantage of opportunities to receive training to increase your knowledge in a particular area while in college or on the job. Adopt a passion for learning new things. Stretch yourself beyond your comfort zone and continue to pursue knowledge to become a life-long learner.

TO THE PARENTS - AFTER ACCEPTANCE

Once your student is admitted and on campus you will feel somewhat of a sense of relief coupled with a bit of anxiety. Although this might be a new experience to you, hopefully you can rest a little bit easier knowing that your student is on their way to fulfilling their dream of attending college. You have helped them in their college search journey thus far and your help has been invaluable. Your student has been admitted to college, they have applied for financial aid and possibly received financial help, they have a residence hall room in which to reside and they have food to eat daily. Allow your mind to rest a bit.

Please realize that the future is now up to them. You should feel confident that they are up to the task. Now is the time to let them go, allowing them to become responsible and manage their own future. You have taken care of them and provided oversight as a parent teaching them survival skills along the way. Allow them to draw upon what you have taught them and to live on their own, satisfied that even if they make mistakes, they will be able to overcome and learn from them. Know that they are responsible young adults capable of great things. Remain accessible but do not hover over them. You might want to set up a weekly check-in time with them so they know that even though they are on their own, you are interested in their lives. Allow them to make decisions and deal with the consequences of those decisions, whether positive or negative. Allow your student to experience life on their own, to make their own way while you remain available should they need help along the way.

You have done an awesome job as a parent. Trust that your student is capable of completing this next phase of their life. Let go and let them stand on their own. Your student is well able to survive and thrive in their college environment. Best wishes to you and to your student, for a bright, productive and successful future!

TO THE STUDENT - AFTER ACCEPTANCE

This book contains many tips that will help you on your journey in pursuit of higher education. Your success though begins in your mind. As you incorporate strategies to become organized and get acclimated to your new surroundings, know that you can do this! Believe in yourself and your ability. Although you might be facing some unfamiliarity and may be a bit nervous about what lies ahead, be confident in your ability to pursue a higher education. There is a bit of weight on you to be successful as a first-year student, especially if you are the first in your family to go to college (FGCS). Get organized and take one day at a time. Put forth your best effort from the very first day. Go to class, seek out friends, join organizations, get to know your professors and seek help from the many people on campus who are employed to support you as you pursue your degree. It is perfectly fine (and smart) to ask for help when you need it.

Remember, you will need to become responsible for your actions and manage your time, health, finances and your academic load. You will need to consistently do the right thing and make good decisions! You are up to the task. Remember to schedule time for rest, relaxation and exercise as well as study time. You will need to balance your load. Pay attention to your physical and psychological health. If you follow the tips in this book and incorporate the good values you have learned at home, you will do well. You are not alone and you are capable of completing this task.

This is the beginning of your "adulting" phase, meaning you will need to make decisions for yourself, often without consulting anyone else, to effectively reach your goals. If you find that you have difficulty achieving your goals, try using some sort of reward system as motivation (Blerkom, 2004). Be responsible for your actions and deal with the consequences of them. Ask for help when you need it and connect with professors and others who can help you along the way. Help others who follow behind you by being a mentor. There are other students coming along who will be looking to you as an example. Be your own motivator and plan your academic course load with your advisor. Make informed decisions. Try your hardest and always give your best effort. If you fall down, get back up and continue on your path learning from any mistakes you have made. I believe in you. Believe in yourself and go for the prize!

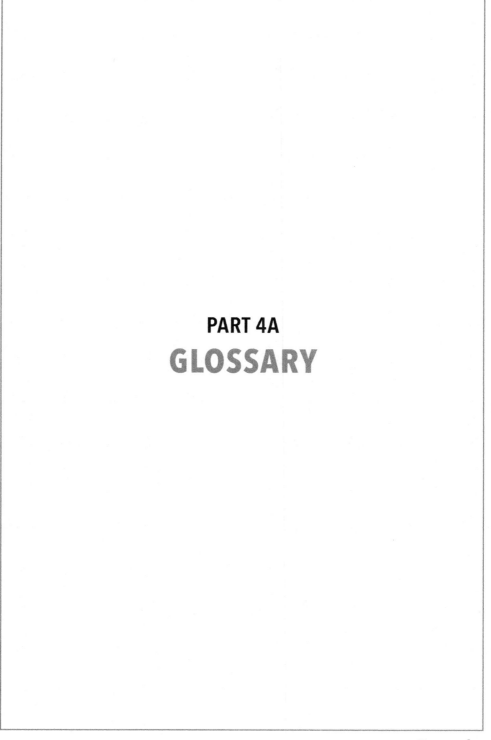

PART 4A
GLOSSARY

ADVISING

the process between the student and an academic advisor of an institution or specific department within an institution that reviews the services and courses offered at the institution, discusses educational plans and upcoming course selections

ACADEMIC ADVISOR

university employee who meets with students to aid in choosing courses and making academic decisions relating to their education

ACCREDITATION

process of validation in which colleges, universities and other institutions of higher learning are evaluated to see if the institutions meet certain levels of competency, authority and quality

ACT

a standardized test used for college admissions in the United States; currently administered by ACT, a nonprofit organization of the same name; test covers several academic skill areas: English, mathematics, reading, science, reasoning and an optional writing test

ADVOCATE

one who supports or promotes the interests of a cause or group

ADULTING

an informal term to describe behavior that is seen as responsible and grown-up

AP (ADVANCED PLACEMENT)

a program in the United States and Canada created by the College Board which offers a college-level curriculum and examinations to high school students. American colleges and universities may grant placement and course credit to students who obtain high scores on the examinations, allowing the students to be exempt from taking specific courses in a sequence and being placed in a higher-level course based upon the score they received

■ APPLICATION FEE

an added cost associated with submitting an application for consideration at a higher education institution

■ APPLICATION FEE WAIVER

allows a student to apply to a higher education institution without paying an application fee

■ AWARD LETTER

the documentation sent from an institution to a student that outlines the amount of financial support the student is eligible to receive

■ CLIMATE

a measure of the real or perceived quality of interpersonal, academic, and professional interactions on a campus and consists of "the current attitudes, behaviors, and standards of faculty, staff, administrators and students concerning the level of respect for individual needs, abilities, and potential" (Rankin & Reason, 2008)

■ COHORT

subdivision of the students in a class or academic department who are at the same level academically

■ COMMON APPLICATION

an undergraduate application that applicants may use to apply to any of more than 800 member colleges and universities in 49 states and the District of Columbia and several foreign countries (not all colleges/universities accept the Common Application)

■ COMMUNITY COLLEGE

two-year institutions providing lower-level tertiary education (continuing education) that grant certificates of program completion, diplomas and associate degrees

■ COST OF ATTENDANCE (COA)

the average annual total amount needed to attend a college or university

DISCRETIONARY EXPENSES
bills resulting from the purchase of items that are not necessary for survival

FAFSA (FREE APPLICATION FOR FEDERAL STUDENT AID)
a form used to apply for financial aid (grants, work-study and loans) to pay for college or career school

FWS (FEDERAL WORK STUDY)
a federal program that allows a student to earn money through various job opportunities at their university

FGCS (FIRST GENERATION COLLEGE STUDENT)
a student who is the first in their family to attend college, or the first to potentially graduate with a degree from college

FINANCIAL NEED
the Cost of Attendance (COA) minus the Expected Family Contribution (EFC)

FYE (FIRST-YEAR EXPERIENCE)
a university program designed to help students survive the first year of college

FIT
how well a student fits in the university setting

FIXED EXPENSES
bills in which the amount due is the same from month to month

FULL-RIDE
a scholarship (does not have to be repaid) that covers tuition, fees and other educational expenses.; may be for a year or renewable over the course of four years

GENERAL EDUCATION REQUIREMENTS
courses that all students must complete regardless of major

GLO (Greek Letter Organization)
sororities and fraternities, social organizations at colleges and universities

GPA (GRADE POINT AVERAGE)
numerical value for letter grades received by assigning each a numeric value and averaging the numbers providing an overall average of all courses taken

GRANT
a type of financial aid that does not have to be repaid in most circumstances

HBCU (HISTORICALLY BLACK COLLEGE OR UNIVERSITY)
an institution that was founded for the education of African Americans at a time when they were banned from enrolling in other educational institutions in the United States

INTERNATIONAL BACCALAUREATE (IB) PROGRAM
a two-year educational curriculum that includes specialized courses for designated students between the ages of 16-19; program provides an internationally accepted qualification for college entry recognized by many universities all over the world

LEGACY ADMIT
preference given to certain applicants based on their familial relationship to alumni of an institution

LOAN
money that is borrowed either from public or private sources that must be repaid over time, with interest

MAJOR
a student's chosen primary academic discipline during their undergraduate studies

MATRICULATE
to be enrolled in a college or university

MENTORSHIP
relationship in which a more experienced or more knowledgeable person helps to guide a less experienced or less knowledgeable person

MINOR
a student's chosen secondary academic discipline during their undergraduate studies

NET INCOME
total income minus total expenses

PERSISTENCE
continued enrollment or degree completion at a college or university

PERSONAL BUDGET
a plan for saving and spending

PWI (PREDOMINANTLY WHITE INSTITUTION)
institutions of higher learning in which white people account for 50% or greater of the student enrollment; also can be historically white

PRIVATE INSTITUTIONS
a school that relies on income from private donations, from religious or other organizations and student tuition

PUBLIC INSTITUTION
a school that receives funding from the state or other governmental entities and that is administered by public boards

RIGOR
the academic or intellectual challenge of a class

SAT
a standardized test widely used for college admissions in the United States that is

intended to assess students' readiness for college. Areas tested include, writing, critical reading and mathematics

SAT FEE WAIVER
allows a student to register for the SAT or an SAT Subject Test free of charge

SCHOLARSHIPS
funds awarded to students based on affiliations, academic achievement or need

SCORE
the nation's largest network of volunteer, expert business mentors

SENIORITIS
an informal term for an affliction of students in their senior year of high school or college, characterized by a decline in motivation or performance

STUDENT ADVOCATE
a member of a school faculty who works with students to ensure they get the help and resources they need to engage in a positive learning experience

SYLLABUS
an outline of the subjects in a course of study

TIME MANAGEMENT
the predictable control an individual can exercise over a series of events by planning to manage tasks at allocated times

TRANSITION
the period of time in which a student endeavors to get acclimated to the college setting

TRADE SCHOOL
a post-secondary institution that provides students with specific technical skills in preparation for a particular occupation

■ TRANSFERABLE COURSES

when credits/hours for courses successfully completed at one university are able to be transferred and counted at a different university toward degree completion

■ UNDERGRADUATE STUDENT

a student who is pursuing a one-, two-, or four-year degree

■ VARIABLE EXPENSES

bills in which the amount due varies from month to month

ABOUT THE AUTHOR

Holding an undergraduate degree in Business Education from Bowling Green State University, a Master of Education degree in Adult Learning and Development from Cleveland State University, and a Doctoral Degree in Higher Education from Ohio University, Dr. Greta Thomas Oliver is a professional coach specializing in student development and is devoted to helping students successfully transition from high school to higher education.

Having spent many years of her life in the classroom as a student as well as a teacher, Greta is a true educator and a supporter of students of all ages. Helping students reach their goals, serving as a resource to help them and their parents navigate the path to college, and making a difference in their lives are her passions.

With over 25 years of experience working with and on behalf of students, her areas of expertise include program development and administration, student recruitment, student retention, career preparation and student development.

Greta is the owner of Greta Oliver Consulting, a hands-on consulting business that specializes in the transition to college, personal development, and career training. To find out more, visit www.GretaOliverConsulting.com.

Greta is the parent of four children, all of whom experienced their own college search/going process. She resides in Chapel Hill, North Carolina as an empty nester with her husband, Terence.

Connect with Greta on these social media platforms:
LinkedIn - http://linkedin.com/in/greta-oliver-ph-d-95244523
Facebook - https://www.facebook.com/gretaoliverconsulting

SPECIAL GIFT FROM DR. OLIVER

Choosing a college and going away to school can be confusing and stressful for both parents and the student.

Now that you've read this book, you're armed with what you need to know about finding a college that fits, what to do as you are waiting for admission decisions, how to set yourself up for success, where to ask for help on campus, and how to navigate the journey from prospective college student to college graduate. The tips provided in this book are for both prospective students and their families and will enable each of you to understand the process and stay organized throughout the journey.

You'll also receive the special bonus I created to add to your toolkit, the Roadmap Essentials, which are 5 downloadable forms that will prove invaluable during college visits, as you work to secure financial aid, and as you compare one institution with another.

While these working papers are offered for sale, as a special bonus you can claim it for free at https://www.gretaoliverconsulting.com/gift

The sooner you apply the essential tips inside this book, the better your chances for successfully creating and following your personal roadmap to higher education success.

I'm in your corner. Let me know if I can help further.

Here's to finding your way through this key process with more ease and less stress.

Best,

PART 4B
WORKING PAPERS

FAFSA IMPORTANT CODES AND LOGIN INFORMATION

Remember you will need to fill out a FAFSA application for all students in your family at the appropriate time each year. Use this form to keep a record of all the information needed to be used from year to year.

PROSPECTIVE STUDENT(1)
FEDERAL STUDENT ID   _____

PIN   _____

SS#   _____

PROSPECTIVE STUDENT(2)
FEDERAL STUDENT ID   _____

PIN   _____

SS#   _____

PROSPECTIVE STUDENT(3)
FEDERAL STUDENT ID   _____

PIN   _____

SS#   _____

PROSPECTIVE STUDENT(4)
FEDERAL STUDENT ID   _____

PIN   _____

SS#   _____

PARENT
FEDERAL STUDENT ID   _____

PIN   _____

FAFSA IMPORTANT CODES AND LOGIN INFORMATION

Remember you will need to fill out a FAFSA application for all students in your family at the appropriate time each year. Use this form to keep a record of all the information needed to be used from year to year.

PROSPECTIVE STUDENT(1)

FEDERAL STUDENT ID _____

PIN _____

SS# _____

PROSPECTIVE STUDENT(2)

FEDERAL STUDENT ID _____

PIN _____

SS# _____

PROSPECTIVE STUDENT(3)

FEDERAL STUDENT ID _____

PIN _____

SS# _____

PROSPECTIVE STUDENT(4)

FEDERAL STUDENT ID _____

PIN _____

SS# _____

PARENT

FEDERAL STUDENT ID _____

PIN _____

COLLEGE VISIT QUESTIONNAIRE AND RESEARCH SHEET - PART A

Institution _____

If you are seriously considering an institution and have not found the answers to these questions in advance by viewing the university website and Fact Book, here are some general questions to ask while on campus:

1. How many volumes are in the library?

2. How many major degree programs does the university offer? (make sure your area of interest is available)

3. What is the average education level of the professors who teach at the university?

4. How much is spent on research at the university?

5. What is the average class size?

6. What is the faculty to student ratio?

7. What is the retention rate between the first and second year?

8. How many students receive accommodations?

9. What celebrations are hosted (recognized) by the institution?

10. Is there a no tuition rate increase guarantee in place at the university?

11. What percentage of students receive financial aid at the university?

12. How many undergraduate students attend the university?

13. Are freshmen students required to reside on campus?

14. When is the freshmen move-in date?

15. When is the freshmen orientation date?

COLLEGE VISIT QUESTIONNAIRE AND RESEARCH SHEET - PART B
College Visit - Assessing the Climate:

Institution _____

Since you are looking for "fit" on campus you will need to pay very close to your feelings while on your campus visit. Look on the university website and see if any climate studies have been recently completed at the university you are visiting in advance of your visit. Once you arrive on campus, here are some questions to consider as you participate in your college visit?

1.   What did you feel when you were on campus?

2.   How would you rate interactions between staff and students on campus?

3.   Were the students friendly?

4.   Did you feel like you were at home on campus?

5.   Were there any activities that interested you? If so, what were they?

6.   What were your opinions regarding the residence halls?

7.   Did you feel safe on campus? Are campus police available?

8.   What is the relationship between town and gown?

9.   What stores are nearby the campus?

10.   What transportation is available?

As you tour the campuses that are of interest to you, keep in mind that you are picking your home for at least the next four years. Trust your gut! Talk to people. Take in your surroundings.

https://www.forbes.com/sites/noodleeducation/2017/02/08/20-things-for-your-college-visit-checklist/#4147ced24723

COLLEGE VISIT QUESTIONNAIRE AND RESEARCH SHEET - PART A

Institution _____

If you are seriously considering an institution and have not found the answers to these questions in advance by viewing the university website and Fact Book, here are some general questions to ask while on campus:

1. How many volumes are in the library?

2. How many major degree programs does the university offer? (make sure your area of interest is available)

3. What is the average education level of the professors who teach at the university?

4. How much is spent on research at the university?

5. What is the average class size?

6. What is the faculty to student ratio?

7. What is the retention rate between the first and second year?

8. How many students receive accommodations?

9. What celebrations are hosted (recognized) by the institution?

10. Is there a no tuition rate increase guarantee in place at the university?

11. What percentage of students receive financial aid at the university?

12. How many undergraduate students attend the university?

13. Are freshmen students required to reside on campus?

14. When is the freshmen move-in date?

15. When is the freshmen orientation date?

COLLEGE VISIT QUESTIONNAIRE AND RESEARCH SHEET - PART B
College Visit - Assessing the Climate:

Institution _____

Since you are looking for "fit" on campus you will need to pay very close to your feelings while on your campus visit. Look on the university website and see if any climate studies have been recently completed at the university you are visiting in advance of your visit. Once you arrive on campus, here are some questions to consider as you participate in your college visit?

1.   What did you feel when you were on campus?

2.   How would you rate interactions between staff and students on campus?

3.   Were the students friendly?

4.   Did you feel like you were at home on campus?

5.   Were there any activities that interested you? If so, what were they?

6.   What were your opinions regarding the residence halls?

7.   Did you feel safe on campus? Are campus police available?

8.   What is the relationship between town and gown?

9.   What stores are nearby the campus?

10.   What transportation is available?

As you tour the campuses that are of interest to you, keep in mind that you are picking your home for at least the next four years. Trust your gut! Talk to people. Take in your surroundings.

https://www.forbes.com/sites/noodleeducation/2017/02/08/20-things-for-your-college-visit-checklist/#4147ced24723

COLLEGE VISIT QUESTIONNAIRE AND RESEARCH SHEET - PART A

Institution _____

If you are seriously considering an institution and have not found the answers to these questions in advance by viewing the university website and Fact Book, here are some general questions to ask while on campus:

1. How many volumes are in the library?

2. How many major degree programs does the university offer? (make sure your area of interest is available)

3. What is the average education level of the professors who teach at the university?

4. How much is spent on research at the university?

5. What is the average class size?

6. What is the faculty to student ratio?

7. What is the retention rate between the first and second year?

8. How many students receive accommodations?

9. What celebrations are hosted (recognized) by the institution?

10. Is there a no tuition rate increase guarantee in place at the university?

11. What percentage of students receive financial aid at the university?

12. How many undergraduate students attend the university?

13. Are freshmen students required to reside on campus?

14. When is the freshmen move-in date?

15. When is the freshmen orientation date?

COLLEGE VISIT QUESTIONNAIRE AND RESEARCH SHEET - PART B
College Visit - Assessing the Climate:

Institution _____

Since you are looking for "fit" on campus you will need to pay very close to your feelings while on your campus visit. Look on the university website and see if any climate studies have been recently completed at the university you are visiting in advance of your visit. Once you arrive on campus, here are some questions to consider as you participate in your college visit?

1.   What did you feel when you were on campus?

2.   How would you rate interactions between staff and students on campus?

3.   Were the students friendly?

4.   Did you feel like you were at home on campus?

5.   Were there any activities that interested you? If so, what were they?

6.   What were your opinions regarding the residence halls?

7.   Did you feel safe on campus? Are campus police available?

8.   What is the relationship between town and gown?

9.   What stores are nearby the campus?

10.   What transportation is available?

As you tour the campuses that are of interest to you, keep in mind that you are picking your home for at least the next four years. Trust your gut! Talk to people. Take in your surroundings.

https://www.forbes.com/sites/noodleeducation/2017/02/08/20-things-for-your-college-visit-checklist/#4147ced24723

COLLEGE APPLICATION CHECKLIST

Print and use this checklist to keep track of your college application requirements, tasks, and deadlines.

COLLEGE:_____

Create a balanced list of reach, match, and safety colleges	☐
Get the application	☐
Make a note of the regular application deadline	☐
Make a note of the early application deadline	☐
Request high school transcript sent	☐
Request midyear grade report sent	☐
Find out if an admission test is required	☐
Take an admission test, if required	☐
Take other required tests (e.g., SAT Subject Tests™, AP Exams, IB exams)	☐
Send admission-test scores	☐
Send other test scores	☐
Request recommendation letters	☐
Send thank-you notes to recommendation writers	☐
Draft initial essay	☐
Proofread essay for spelling and grammar	☐
Have two people read your essay	☐
Revise your essay	☐
Proofread your revision	☐

COLLEGE APPLICATION CHECKLIST (cont'd)

- Interview at college campus ☐
- Have an alumni interview ☐
- Submit FAFSA® ☐
- Submit PROFILE, if needed ☐
- Make a note of the priority financial aid deadline ☐
- Make a note of the regular financial aid deadline ☐
- Complete college application ☐
- Make copies of all application materials ☐
- Pay application fee ☐
- Sign and send application ☐
- Submit college aid form, if needed ☐
- Submit state aid form, if needed ☐
- Confirm receipt of application materials ☐
- Send additional material, if needed ☐
- Tell school counselor that you applied ☐
- Receive letter from office of admission ☐
- Receive financial aid award letter ☐
- Meet deadline to accept admission and send deposit ☐
- Accept financial aid offer ☐
- Notify the colleges you will not attend ☐

COLLEGE APPLICATION CHECKLIST

Print and use this checklist to keep track of your college application requirements, tasks, and deadlines.

COLLEGE:_____

- [ ] Create a balanced list of reach, match, and safety colleges
- [ ] Get the application
- [ ] Make a note of the regular application deadline
- [ ] Make a note of the early application deadline
- [ ] Request high school transcript sent
- [ ] Request midyear grade report sent
- [ ] Find out if an admission test is required
- [ ] Take an admission test, if required
- [ ] Take other required tests (e.g., SAT Subject Tests™, AP Exams, IB exams)
- [ ] Send admission-test scores
- [ ] Send other test scores
- [ ] Request recommendation letters
- [ ] Send thank-you notes to recommendation writers
- [ ] Draft initial essay
- [ ] Proofread essay for spelling and grammar
- [ ] Have two people read your essay
- [ ] Revise your essay
- [ ] Proofread your revision

COLLEGE APPLICATION CHECKLIST (cont'd)

- Interview at college campus ☐
- Have an alumni interview ☐
- Submit FAFSA® ☐
- Submit PROFILE, if needed ☐
- Make a note of the priority financial aid deadline ☐
- Make a note of the regular financial aid deadline ☐
- Complete college application ☐
- Make copies of all application materials ☐
- Pay application fee ☐
- Sign and send application ☐
- Submit college aid form, if needed ☐
- Submit state aid form, if needed ☐
- Confirm receipt of application materials ☐
- Send additional material, if needed ☐
- Tell school counselor that you applied ☐
- Receive letter from office of admission ☐
- Receive financial aid award letter ☐
- Meet deadline to accept admission and send deposit ☐
- Accept financial aid offer ☐
- Notify the colleges you will not attend ☐

COLLEGE APPLICATION CHECKLIST

Print and use this checklist to keep track of your college application requirements, tasks, and deadlines.

COLLEGE:_____

Create a balanced list of reach, match, and safety colleges	☐
Get the application	☐
Make a note of the regular application deadline	☐
Make a note of the early application deadline	☐
Request high school transcript sent	☐
Request midyear grade report sent	☐
Find out if an admission test is required	☐
Take an admission test, if required	☐
Take other required tests (e.g., SAT Subject Tests™, AP Exams, IB exams)	☐
Send admission-test scores	☐
Send other test scores	☐
Request recommendation letters	☐
Send thank-you notes to recommendation writers	☐
Draft initial essay	☐
Proofread essay for spelling and grammar	☐
Have two people read your essay	☐
Revise your essay	☐
Proofread your revision	☐

COLLEGE APPLICATION CHECKLIST (cont'd)

Interview at college campus ☐

Have an alumni interview ☐

Submit FAFSA® ☐

Submit PROFILE, if needed ☐

Make a note of the priority financial aid deadline ☐

Make a note of the regular financial aid deadline ☐

Complete college application ☐

Make copies of all application materials ☐

Pay application fee ☐

Sign and send application ☐

Submit college aid form, if needed ☐

Submit state aid form, if needed ☐

Confirm receipt of application materials ☐

Send additional material, if needed ☐

Tell school counselor that you applied ☐

Receive letter from office of admission ☐

Receive financial aid award letter ☐

Meet deadline to accept admission and send deposit ☐

Accept financial aid offer ☐

Notify the colleges you will not attend ☐

SCHOLARSHIP TRACKER

Use this to keep track of your scholarship application requirements, tasks, deadlines and progress.

SCHOLARSHIP NAME: _____

DEADLINE DATE: _____

AMOUNT OF AWARD: _____

APPLICATION DATE: _____

NOTES: _____

_____

STATUS: _____

SCHOLARSHIP TRACKER

Use this to keep track of your scholarship application requirements, tasks, deadlines and progress.

SCHOLARSHIP NAME: _____

DEADLINE DATE: _____

AMOUNT OF AWARD: _____

APPLICATION DATE: _____

NOTES: _____

_____

STATUS: _____

SCHOLARSHIP TRACKER

Use this to keep track of your scholarship application requirements, tasks, deadlines and progress.

SCHOLARSHIP NAME: _____

DEADLINE DATE: _____

AMOUNT OF AWARD: _____

APPLICATION DATE: _____

NOTES: _____

_____

STATUS: _____

SCHOLARSHIP TRACKER

Use this to keep track of your scholarship application requirements, tasks, deadlines and progress.

SCHOLARSHIP NAME: _____

DEADLINE DATE: _____

AMOUNT OF AWARD: _____

APPLICATION DATE: _____

NOTES: _____

_____

STATUS: _____

DAILY PLANNING WORKSHEET

DATE _____

	TASKS	DONE	APPTS	DONE	OTHER	DONE
7AM						
8AM						
9AM						
10AM						
11AM						
12PM						
1PM						
2PM						
3PM						
4PM						
5PM						
6PM						
7PM						
8PM						
9PM						
10PM						
11PM						
12AM						

DAILY PLANNING WORKSHEET

DATE _____

	TASKS	DONE	APPTS	DONE	OTHER	DONE
7AM						
8AM						
9AM						
10AM						
11AM						
12PM						
1PM						
2PM						
3PM						
4PM						
5PM						
6PM						
7PM						
8PM						
9PM						
10PM						
11PM						
12AM						

DAILY PLANNING WORKSHEET

DATE _____

	TASKS	DONE	APPTS	DONE	OTHER	DONE
7AM						
8AM						
9AM						
10AM						
11AM						
12PM						
1PM						
2PM						
3PM						
4PM						
5PM						
6PM						
7PM						
8PM						
9PM						
10PM						
11PM						
12AM						

TIME MANAGEMENT PLANNING SHEET

PRIORITY #	DATE	PRIORITIZED DAILY TASK LIST	NOTES

TIME MANAGEMENT PLANNING SHEET

PRIORITY #	DATE	PRIORITIZED DAILY TASK LIST	NOTES

PERSONAL BUDGETING

	JAN	FEB	MAR	APR	MAY	JUN	JUL	AUG	SEP	OCT	NOV	DEC	TOTAL	AVG
INCOME														
Wages & Tips														
Allowance														
Gifts														
Other monies														
Refunds/Reimbursements														
Transfer from Savings														
Other														
TOTAL INCOME PER MONTH														
EXPENSES														
Phone														
Books														
Food														
Supplies														
Transportation														
Gas														
Entertainment														
Transfer to Savings														
Loans														
Credit Card(s)														
Miscellaneous														
Other														
TOTAL EXPENSES PER MONTH														

NET INCOME = TOTAL INCOME - TOTAL EXPENSES

PERSONAL BUDGETING

	JAN	FEB	MAR	APR	MAY	JUN	JUL	AUG	SEP	OCT	NOV	DEC	TOTAL	AVG
INCOME														
Wages & Tips														
Allowance														
Gifts														
Other monies														
Refunds/Reimbursements														
Transfer from Savings														
Other														
TOTAL INCOME PER MONTH														
EXPENSES														
Phone														
Books														
Food														
Supplies														
Transportation														
Gas														
Entertainment														
Transfer to Savings														
Loans														
Credit Card(s)														
Miscellaneous														
Other														
TOTAL EXPENSES PER MONTH														

NET INCOME = TOTAL INCOME - TOTAL EXPENSES

PERSONAL BUDGETING

	JAN	FEB	MAR	APR	MAY	JUN	JUL	AUG	SEP	OCT	NOV	DEC	TOTAL	AVG
INCOME														
Wages & Tips														
Allowance														
Gifts														
Other monies														
Refunds/Reimbursements														
Transfer from Savings														
Other														
TOTAL INCOME PER MONTH														
EXPENSES														
Phone														
Books														
Food														
Supplies														
Transportation														
Gas														
Entertainment														
Transfer to Savings														
Loans														
Credit Card(s)														
Miscellaneous														
Other														
TOTAL EXPENSES PER MONTH														

NET INCOME = TOTAL INCOME - TOTAL EXPENSES

PERSONAL BUDGETING

	JAN	FEB	MAR	APR	MAY	JUN	JUL	AUG	SEP	OCT	NOV	DEC	TOTAL	AVG
INCOME														
Wages & Tips														
Allowance														
Gifts														
Other monies														
Refunds/Reimbursements														
Transfer from Savings														
Other														
TOTAL INCOME PER MONTH														
EXPENSES														
Phone														
Books														
Food														
Supplies														
Transportation														
Gas														
Entertainment														
Transfer to Savings														
Loans														
Credit Card(s)														
Miscellaneous														
Other														
TOTAL EXPENSES PER MONTH														

NET INCOME = TOTAL INCOME - TOTAL EXPENSES

PERSONAL BUDGETING

	JAN	FEB	MAR	APR	MAY	JUN	JUL	AUG	SEP	OCT	NOV	DEC	TOTAL	AVG
INCOME														
Wages & Tips														
Allowance														
Gifts														
Other monies														
Refunds/Reimbursements														
Transfer from Savings														
Other														
TOTAL INCOME PER MONTH														
EXPENSES														
Phone														
Books														
Food														
Supplies														
Transportation														
Gas														
Entertainment														
Transfer to Savings														
Loans														
Credit Card(s)														
Miscellaneous														
Other														
TOTAL EXPENSES PER MONTH														

NET INCOME = TOTAL INCOME - TOTAL EXPENSES

REFERENCES

Are the Cost Differences Between In-State and Out-of-State Colleges? (n.d.). Retrieved from https://bigfuture.collegeboard.org/.

Blerkom, D. L. (2004). Orientation to College Learning. California: Wadsworth/Thompson.

Camden, W. (1636). Remaines Concerning Britaine. (5). Retrieved from https://quoteinvestigator.com.

Carmichael, M. (2012, September 24). What is the Clery Act? Boston Globe. Https://www.bostonglobe.com/.

College application checklist. (n.d.). Retrieved and adapted from https://bigfuture.collegeboard.org/.

Davis, B. G. (2009). Tools for Teaching. (2). California: Jossey-Bass.

How Fastweb Works (n.d.) Retrieved from www.fastweb.com.

FAFSA Application. (n.d.). Retrieved from https://studentaid.gov/h/apply-for-aid/fafsa.

Fall 2016 Headcount Enrollment. (n.d.). Retrieved from https://oira.unc.edu/.

Federal Student Aid: Find the Information You Need (n.d.). Retrieved from https://studentaid.gov/sites/default/files/federal-student-aid-info-online.pdf.

Light, R. J. (2001). Making the Most of College: Students Speak Their Minds. Massachusetts: Harvard University Press.

Rankin, S., & Reason, R. (2008). Transformational tapestry model: A comprehensive approach to transforming campus climate. Journal of Diversity in Higher Education, 1(4), 262-274.

Riffe, Florence (2021). Application essay concept adapted.

Things for your college visit checklist. (n.d.). Retrieved and adapted from https://www.forbes.com/.

Wake Technical Community College (2015, August). Time management, budgeting, learning styles, stress and mental health concepts adapted from Human Resource Department curriculum.

NOTES

Made in the USA
Middletown, DE
25 January 2022

59297315R00076